Videostyle in Senate Campaigns

VIDEOSTYLE

IN SENATE CAMPAIGNS

Dorothy Davidson Nesbit

The University of Tennessee Press / Knoxville

Copyright © 1988 by The University of Tennessee Press / Knoxville.
All Rights Reserved. Manufactured in the United States of America.
First Edition.

The paper in this book meets the minimum requirements of the
American National Standard for Permanence of Paper for Printed
Library Materials. ∞   The binding materials have been chosen
for strength and durability.

Library of Congress Cataloging-in-Publication Data

Nesbit, Dorothy Davidson, 1956–
  Videostyle in Senate campaigns.

  Bibliography: p.
  Includes index.
  1. Television in politics—United States—Case
studies.   2. Advertising, Political—United States
—Case studies.   3. United States. Congress. Senate
—Elections—Case studies.   I. Title.
HE8700.76.U6N47   1988   324.7′3′0973   88-2166
ISBN 0-87049-582-8 (alk. paper)

This book is dedicated to my husband, Phillip F. Nesbit, who taught me all about the finer points of courtship in the most meaningful way.

Contents

Acknowledgments

This book could not have been written without the frank and open cooperation of three U.S. senators, the candidates challenging them for reelection, and the media advisors who produced the campaign spots. I am especially grateful to them for sharing their insights, triumphs, and disappointments. Because of their honesty in responding to my questions, I left the interviews with a deeper understanding of the electoral process, and much empathy for those who subject themselves and their families to the rigors of courting the public. I can only hope that I have done justice to their stories.

This project has been a lengthy one, and thus the list of friends who have encouraged and supported this work over the past five years is also lengthy. My graduate school colleagues, Paul Lopatto, and Yvette Nowak, Jim Stimson, Richard Eichenberg, and Russ Dalton, shared my enthusiasm over the idea and gave me that initial push to begin. Mavis Bryant, an editor at the University of Tennessee Press, encouraged the writing of this book based on a paper I presented at the Southwestern Social Science Association meeting as a graduate student. Knowing there was interest made the writing much easier.

Many colleagues at Oklahoma University also offered support. Don Kash supported my efforts to get funding from the University Research Council, successfully, and the National Science Foundation, not so successfully. Gary Copeland read the manuscript in one of its previous incarnations. I am most especially grateful to Ken Hoving and the Oklahoma University Research Council for providing the travel funds necessary to conduct the interviews, and to Jim Burwell and the Oklahoma University College of Arts and Sciences for a summer fellowship which allowed me time to work on the conceptualization of the project.

The political science departments at the University of Minnesota and the University of New Mexico generously provided a quiet haven in which to write for the summers of 1984 and 1985 respectively. Phil Shively, Paul Hain, and Chris Garcia generously listened to my writing struggles and helped me gain perspective when the task loomed too large. The Center for Governmental Studies at Northern Illinois University provided financial support for copying videotapes, conference travel to present two papers on videostyle, and a place to write without interruption in the summer of 1986. Bob Blank read and commented on a version of the manuscript. Terri Silvius worked late at night and weekends producing a final manuscript. Her expertise and good humor are much appreciated.

Several other colleagues played major roles in supporting and encouraging this work. Paul Allen Beck read early drafts of several chapters, greatly improving their construction and conceptualization. I know the multiple roles he has played over the last five years have not been easy, but he is without equal as mentor. Edie Goldenberg offered much in the way of helpful advice, and for her insights I am extremely grateful. Doris Graber read and commented on an early version of the manuscript. More than that, she was an expert listener, and sympathetic colleague, as well as role model. She has my affection and highest regard. Dear friends, Jeff and Nancy Brudney, Kent Jennings, and Maurine Patten, offered much encouragement at critical junctures.

1

Introduction

Harold Doright had returned to the state after a fairly long absence devoted to nonpolitical public service. Though very successful, he was not well known. In early May, a TV spot was aired to introduce Hal Doright to the people of the state. The audio portion of the ad featured an announcer's voice talking about this political newcomer's goals for the state, his commitment to and compassion for the people of the state; and his qualifications for office. There were several references to Hal's impressive accomplishments outside politics. The tagline, amid the rousing sound of applause and cheers: "We announce with pride, Harold Doright for United States Senate."

The pictures that accompany the announcer's voice begin with a long shot of a mesa with the sun rising over a mountain in the background. The candidate is walking toward the camera, dressed in slacks, leather jacket, and bolo tie. As he walks forward, the camera moves in for a close-up of his face. Cut to a sequence of shots of the candidate with all kinds of people—young, old, men, women, children. The people are gathering around him, reaching out to touch him, shake his hand. Two children run up to him smiling, stop (suddenly shy), and, still smiling, look up at him. Cut to another sequence, a picture of a convention hall filled with people wearing white straw hats and carrying red, white, and blue banners and posters with the candidate's name and picture. As the candidate walks through the crowd, they are cheering and waving the posters of him. He takes the podium and begins to speak as the camera moves in for a final close-up.

Still other information is communicated which is neither verbal nor visual. There is music in the background, noticeable beneath the announcer's strong masculine voice. It is not the brassy beat of a marching band, but a soft, and at the same time powerful, symphony. It sounds like the theme from some space odyssey—futuristic and at the same time classic. The pace of the cuts between shots and scenes gradually builds with the music to a climax as the camera moves in for that final close-up. Shots of the candidate are always low angle or head on. The candidate's voice is never heard. At the same time it is as if we are on some magic carpet ride, outside the living room, on the road with Hal Doright. The spot is reality, and we are *with* the candidate, part of the crowd of people reaching for him. As he touches them, he touches us. We know him, or at least we think we do, after viewing this two minute spot.

Another state, another race. Senator Niceguy is running for reelection. He has a strong lead going into the race and is generally well thought of throughout the state. One reason for his popularity is the attention he has paid to casework. Although he has never served in Congress, his style seems patterned after the Congressmen who devote more than half of their time and resources to attending the individual needs of their constituents. Throughout the campaign, a spot is aired that deals with one of the cases Matthew Niceguy has helped resolve. The audio portion of the spot features a woman talking about how her son had been kidnapped by his father following a messy divorce and a custody fight that she won. She speaks of her despair and anguish, of not knowing where to turn, and of turning to Senator Niceguy in a desperate attempt to get her son back. In the end she is reunited with her son, and we hear of Senator Niceguy's legislative efforts on behalf of families.

The pictures that accompany the woman's voice begin with a medium shot of the woman speaking. The camera moves back into a long shot revealing her home—the living room. The camera seeks out the photographs of her son placed around the room, his trophies, his baseball glove, finally returning to his mother. Moving in for a close-up, we see the tortured look in her eyes, glistening with tears. We see the emptiness of the room awaiting the boy's return. The heartache of a mother. Now the camera cuts to the son walking up the steps to the house, his mother going out to greet him. She embraces her son. Now we see mother and son together in the living room. The boy goes to a glass-front case and tapes an autographed picture of Senator Niceguy to the glass.

Still other elements of the spot communicate the mood. Again, there is music in the background. Slow, sad, haunting. It is a lone instrument, searching for the right note. The pace of the cuts between shots and scenes is constant, neither fast nor slow. The candidate is never seen, except in the photograph. The candidate's voice is never heard. The woman we hear is obviously not a professional actress. Her voice occasionally cracks and breaks. She is middle-aged, slightly overweight, her face creased with worry. She is clean and neat, and so is her home, but she is also clearly struggling. Not rich. Not poor. This woman could be anyone's neighbor. This tragedy could be anyone's tragedy. It is as if we stopped in at our own next-door neighbor's for a cup of coffee and were treated to a friend's confidence. We are moved to console her, and we are glad that Matt Niceguy is strong and compassionate enough to help our neighbor.

The final race. Senator Cloistered faces a strong challenge from the charming and well-liked Thomas Popular. Throughout his term he has periodically polled his constituents; the incumbent is well aware of his own strengths and liabilities as a candidate. The Achilles heel of his campaign is the public's perception that Senator Cloistered is cold. The senator has arranged to have public opinion tracked throughout the campaign so that he can respond appropriately to constituent concerns. Whenever the polls detect a slight drop in political support, the incumbent airs the spot his producer dubs "hearts and flowers."

The audio portion of this ad features Senator Cloistered reflecting on his job as a senator. His voice is calm, well modulated. He talks about the uniqueness of his state, its people. He talks about his goals for the state, the work he has accomplished so far, the work yet to be done. The substance of what he says deals with his *feelings* about that work, not the solutions to problems, not his positions on issues.

As we listen to Senator Cloistered, we see a medium shot of him seated, jacket off, tie loosened, collar open. He is sitting in his office chair. The camera moves in for a close-up. Then cuts to a series of shots showing the senator at work. He is walking down a hallway of the Senate building, talking with staffers. He is in a committee hearing with other senators. Then he is back home, talking to constituents, shaking hands, listening, answering questions. In each picture we see him with other people. He is standing or seated close to them, often touching a shoulder, shaking a hand. We see him at home, with his wife in the kitchen, surreptitiously feeding his dog a tidbit of something good. We see his children surrounding him, climbing all over him.

There is a subtle undercurrent of music. Soft, melodic, upbeat, but not jazzy. Every shot in the spot features the senator, most of them showing him surrounded by people. Very often the scenes are informal ones—the senator at home with his family, talking with the people of his state, sharing a cup of coffee with miners and construction workers. The pace of the shots is moderate, neither building nor slowing to the close, a final close-up of Senator Cloistered.

These political commercials illustrate the rich information that political spots can convey. In them, the candidates offer views of themselves to the public—often in a setting that implies that the viewer is getting a more intimate glimpse of them than may actually be the case. Political spots are, at their core, the presentations of candidates to audiences. But unlike the interpersonal "presentation of self" described by Goffman and Fenno, the commercial spot is not uniquely determined by the presenter.[1] The spot is the composite result of candidates' self-images, producers' theories about how to market these candidates, and actual political situations. There are vast differences between interactions of individuals interpersonally and interactions mediated by television.

Television has changed the way candidates campaign. To borrow a phrase from Erving Goffman, it has changed "the presentation of self." Scholars have been attempting to pinpoint the effect of media exposure on viewers' perceptions and behaviors since 1952 when the Republicans mounted a media blitz in the last three weeks of the presidential campaign. This book is *not* about the effects of media exposure on the mass public.[2] This book is about the candidates who star in, and the producers who create, the ads. It focuses intensively on three pairs of candidates for the United States Senate and their media consultants.

Despite a now-lengthy research tradition analyzing the impact of television on politics, there is little agreement on

the exact nature of that impact. There is even less agreement
on the appropriate methodology, setting, and theoretical focus for such studies. Television variously has been accused
of creating complacency and passivity in viewers, credited
with increasing voter knowledge and awareness, and dismissed as having no effect whatever. In certain political contexts, under some conditions, any of these conclusions can
be empirically demonstrated.

Whether social scientists agree on if and how to study political television may be less important than the widespread
belief among candidates and political consultants that the
media have an important impact on the public. The pre-
dominance of that belief is reflected in the amount of money
spent on television advertising.[3] However, the amount spent
on television does not necessarily reflect the quality of the
media campaign.[4] In the course of one interview, an unsuccessful candidate for the United States Senate reflected:

> . . . all those mornings of getting up and traveling didn't
> mean anything. I'm convinced that people made up their
> minds watching TV commercials—not even the press cover-
> age. That's where minds are made up in large enough num-
> bers to win elections.[5]

Among the volumes of research findings on media and
politics, we now have survey research that tells us what
channels of communication the public relies on most.[6] We
have experimental studies that link media exposure to attitude change.[7] We have content analyses that tell us what
kinds of information are being communicated through news-
papers, televised news reports, and political advertising.[8] We
have anecdotal books describing the life of the reporter on
the campaign trail.[9] We have narratives on the rise of political consultants, including some by consultants themselves,
documenting their strategies for selling candidates.[10] We
have literature that investigates the effectiveness of legisla-

tion designed to reduce the impact of money spent on televised advertising on elections.[11]

What we do not have is research that looks at the interactions of competing candidates, or the interactions between candidates and their producers, during a campaign.[12] This book asks: "What theories do media producers and candidates have about the electorate? What happens when those theories find themselves in direct competition with each other?"

The conventional approach to understanding the electoral process has been finding out how voters actually make decisions, a process that is still being debated despite more than thirty years of voting research. This book focuses instead on finding out how candidates and consultants *think* voters are reaching their decisions. The assumption is that candidates try to present themselves to voters in terms of characteristics for which they think the voters are looking. Consultants, who produce the ads through which the candidates are presented, also have theories about what the voters want. In any given race then, there are four actors—two candidates and two producers—all with potentially different theories about what the electorate wants. Whose perceptions are reflected in the content of the ads? What happens when different campaign theories find themselves in direct competition? For the political practitioner, the proof of the theory is in the election results. Political careers are built on the ability to win elections. While one loss may be a setback, a loss at the level of the United State Senate is more likely to mean political death. For the political consultant, reputation is prosperity—if not survival. A series of losses is difficult to shrug off. Some races must be won just to stay in the game.

It is the interactions of the campaign principals that are important in understanding the campaign process. It is hardly ever the case that the candidate is running without a thought to what his opponent is doing. It is hardly ever the case that the candidate makes decisions about his political future without trying to get the best information available. Frequently, the "best" information available is defined by the cost of getting that information. Therefore, the candidates seek the advice of high-priced consultants, with one eye always on their opponents.

If we are to gain new insights into the electoral process, if we are to understand the role of the media, if we are to breath new life into the massive election data sets, we must step back and reassess our approach. In stepping back, it becomes clear that among the most neglected foci of the study of electoral politics are the candidates themselves. The data we are most sorely missing are of candidates competing with one another in a single race, in a single political, social, and economic environment. Understanding the candidates' views requires in-depth interviewing. Extensive survey sampling techniques are not well suited to this task. The researcher must get to know the candidates and their races intensively. Intensive analysis complements extensive analysis. Sharpen the focus, ask slightly different questions, and new insights emerge. Intensive analysis, like any single approach, has its weaknesses. Our understanding of political behavior is enhanced by approaching the topic from a variety of angles. The relative inexpensiveness and ease of access to large, quantitative data sets has made that approach flourish. In contrast, it has not been obvious how one should qualitatively evaluate a campaign. The peculiarities of many case studies have prevented them from being used as systematic models of the campaign process. This book uses U.S. Senate races in three states to show how the quality or characteristics of campaigns may be evaluated using a "courtship" perspective.

Richard Fenno's *Home Style* gives us a valuable look at the interaction between members of Congress and their constituents. At the same time, my own experiences in political campaigns suggest that the rules governing the personal interactions that Fenno observes are not readily translated to other modes of communication. When the context of the interaction is mass rather than interpersonal communication, the dynamics are astonishingly different.

This project began in 1980 with a two-case pilot study, analyzing the content of political commercials for two candidates, an incumbent and a challenger, in different races. The content analysis was tantalizing, but not satisfying. For example, upon returning one of the candidates' ads, I asked the producer why party affiliation was never mentioned. His response—"Are you sure?"—implied that the decision not to include partisanship in the ad was *unconscious*, yet most popular writing about political consultants suggests they possess a more Machiavellian mindset.

The pilot study was inspired by *Home Style*, but videostyle was different. The most obvious differences revealed by the content analysis were not sufficient to build a theory on. The data provided by the content analysis only increased the difficulties of defining "videostyle." Content analysis does not reveal why certain production decisions are made, how the ads are aired, or in what sequence. If the object of inquiry is understanding why the candidates portray themselves the way they do, it is imperative to talk to the people involved in making the ads. Interviewing all the principal actors in a race is the only way of transforming the analysis into something more than a tally of bits of information contained in the ads. A number of scholars have analyzed the content of spots, and we have a fairly good idea of the type of information contained in them. Does the presentation of this information possess a certain style? What, or who, determines the style? Are some styles more successful than others?

Videostyle is different from home style, and these differences emanate in part from the different types of communication involved.[13] The interpersonal communication that Fenno observed did not rely on any intermediary to translate messages from candidate to constituent. The mass communication involved in political advertising does. Interpersonal communication involves small, homogeneous audiences. The candidate knows the audience in advance; they are selected deliberately when he chooses to visit the Rotary Club, Jaycees, Farm Bureau, or Chamber of Commerce. Candidate messages may be tailored to audience interests. In televised political advertising, the audience is inadvertent.[14] Viewers are watching the commercial because it leads into or out of a program. The spot message is received by a large, heterogeneous audience. In general, the candidate does not know who is tuned in to his message. The members of his audience may have nothing more in common than the fact that they turned on their TV sets at a given time.

Interpersonal communication involves slow message transmission, shared control of the communication process, and high quality and quantity of feedback. The audience has an opportunity to react to the message. The candidate has an opportunity to modify his speaking rate, or explain in greater detail points of his message that seem to need clarification. In the interpersonal situation, the candidate facing a cool audience can detect their mood and "warm them up" with a joke, with a reference to some local event or personality to show them that he is one of them. It is the characteristics of interpersonal communication that lead us to hypothesize that the ability to "think on your feet" is critical for candidates campaigning face-to-face.

Mass communication involves rapid, simultaneous message transmission. The audience receives the message quickly—typically in thirty to sixty seconds. Each member of the audience receives the message at the same time. Mass communication involves virtually no feedback, and what little feedback may occur is delayed. The immediate response to the message will go undetected. The candidate facing a cool audience through television will not even detect it unless he has arranged some sort of opinion tracking through survey research. He cannot adjust his message immediately to respond to the mood of the audience. The characteristics of mass communication lead us to hypothesize that the ability to *anticipate* the audience's receptivity is more critical than the ability to "think on your feet" for candidates campaigning on television. Television communication requires different skills of a candidate than interpersonal communication. The ability to develop these skills, and the kinds of skills emphasized to win, may spill over and affect performance in office later.[15]

The presentation of self through television is further complicated because, not only is the content of the ad decided by many persons, but so too is the timing, frequency, and sequence of airing the spots. In short, the candidate's presentation of self is no longer uniquely determined by the candidate. Furthermore, the differences in the audience, message control, and message transmission dictate that the elements of videostyle will differ from the elements of Fenno's home style.

Fenno analyzed the interaction between congressmen and their constituents—in the district. He describes congressmen's perceptions of their constituencies as concentric circles. The geographical constituency is the outermost ring. Moving inward are the reelection constituency and the strongest supporters or primary constituency. The political intimates or personal constituency form the innermost ring. For Fenno, home styles are a function of the congressman's perceptions of his constituency. The allocation of resources to the district, the presentation of self, the explanation of Washington activity, and the career stage of the congressman are components of home style.

This book analyzes the interaction between senators and

their constituents, producers, and challengers in the context of televised advertising. The campaign can best be described as a courtship process. Over the course of the campaign (and over the course of a career) the candidates' relationship with constituents potentially passes through five relationship stages: initial attraction, building a relationship, continuation, deterioration, and ending. The candidates' styles of relating to others are apparent in the way they present themselves to others through televised advertising. These presentations of selves—or videostyles—are a function of the political situation of the candidate, the context of the race, and the strategic decisions of actors other than the candidate. An information factor and intimacy factor are key components of videostyle. They can be expressed through the audio, video, or production content of the spot.

Using the framework of the presentation of self, the following chapters take an in-depth look at three Senate races. The points discussed in each chapter also apply to the other races discussed, unless otherwise noted. However, some races provided better illustrative material and for this reason were selected to discuss particular points.

United States Senate races are the setting for this study. Senate races are especially well suited to the study of videostyle. These campaigns rely heavily on television since most states (unlike House districts) contain media market areas for which televised advertising is the most efficient means of reaching large numbers of voters quickly.

Until recently, Senate races have shown sufficient losses by incumbents to suggest likely campaign effects. (In 1982 for the first time, the incumbent return rate for the Senate exceeded the return rate for the House incumbents.)[16] Senate races, unlike presidential contests, provide enough different races to permit comparisons between pairs of candidates running at the same time. This analysis is based on interviews with incumbent senators, their challengers, and the political producers of their campaigns.

This book relies heavily upon the participant observation method (lovingly termed "soaking and poking" by Fenno, and disparagingly called "flopping and floundering" by others). Content analysis alone does not allow one to draw essential conclusions, nor does it provide important information about the underlying strategy of the ads. Thus, the interviews discussed here are a critical element of the analysis.

In order to protect the identities of cooperating individuals, the names of people, places, and sometimes things have been changed. Of course, senators are more difficult to disguise than congressmen, simply because there are fewer of them. Furthermore, some characteristics of videostyle emerged which had explicitly regional connotations. The reader is cautioned against trying to identify particular individuals since some details have been changed to protect identities. The same conclusions about the importance of local culture can be drawn whether the candidate is portrayed as wearing a hardhat or a cowboy hat.

The interviews themselves were free flowing, but contained a core set of questions which all individuals responded to. As anyone who has attempted this type of research knows, interviews find their own rhythms. Some interviewees required extensive probing. In other cases, the interview seemed to provide a welcome catharsis. During the interviews I took extensive notes but did not tape record the conversations. I was afraid a tape recorder would inhibit the natural responses of the interviewee. There is something about facing a microphone that changes the chemistry of the exchange. Following each interview, I wrote extensive notes recording it.

Following the candidates around during the campaign and sitting in on meetings where strategic decisions are being made might have been a preferable research strategy perhaps, but in this instance it would not have worked. First, the races discussed here were over by the time of the interviews, and by the time funding to conduct the interviews was obtained. Second, candidates are unlikely to allow a researcher to listen to strategic discussions on which their careers rest, knowing that the researcher will soon be visiting their challenger's offices. The opportunity of watching the process unfold was eschewed for the opportunity of interviewing all the participants. When the race is over, candidates can afford to discuss their campaigns. There are no more strategic secrets.

The three races described on the first pages of this book were chosen on the basis of: 1) availability of campaign commercials, 2) access to candidates and producers for interviews, and 3) ability to hold constant certain features of the race and contextual variables (party affiliation, region, and the presence of an incumbent in the race). Interviews were conducted between November of 1982 and August of 1984. The interviews lasted between one and three hours. The races described here are not presumed to represent in a random selection sense the wider universe of all Senate races, or even the smaller universe of Senate races in 1982. Interviews are supplemented by the qualitative analysis of the actual campaign spots aired.

Off-year elections, such as 1982, differ from presidential election years in that voter turnout is typically lower. Furthermore, the Senate candidates are heading up the ticket—and this may generate more publicity for them than in presidential election years. Neither of these characteristics should necessarily result in a markedly different *process* of relationship building or presentation of self through television advertising.

While these three races are not representative in the statistical sense, they vividly illustrate a process with which all candidates must wrestle. Regardless of election year, all candidates face the challenges of relationship building or maintenance, and the threat of relationship deterioration. Challengers generally may face hurdles similar to the hurdles faced by the challengers interviewed here in the initial attraction phases of their relationship. Incumbents in other races may experience difficulties similar to those experienced by the incumbents interviewed here in trying to maintain relationships.

Throughout the book the male pronoun and masculine examples have been used. This is not intended to imply that women in politics do not "court" in much the same ways as their male counterparts. Rather, it is a result of the fact that at present there are only two women in the U.S. Senate—both of whom are readily identifiable—and few women political producers. Because this book consists of three case studies using the plural might be misleading, and using the feminine might be too revealing.

Three candidates were interviewed in Washington, D.C. Three were interviewed in the states where the races occurred. Producers were interviewed wherever their offices were—sometimes in the campaign location, sometimes in other areas of the country. Interviews were conducted after the elections; had they been done during the course of the campaign, reactions might have been different. Certainly some rationalizations are to be expected subsequent to an event as all-absorbing as a campaign. In only one instance was the interviewer frustrated by a candidate's responses. Readers can themselves judge the sincerity of responses or whether rapport seems to be lacking, since material from the interviews is quoted at length in the text. The content of the ads is used to illustrate the interview material. To some extent, it helps to overcome the problem of candidate/producer "selective memory" and provides an objective measure of what the ads actually said—how the candidates truly were presented.

Chapter 2 lays out the notion of the courtship campaign and discusses the concept of the presentation of self. Some of the principles of communication are altered in the context of television. Television shapes the expression of videostyle through the audio, video, and production content of the ads.

Chapter 3 analyzes the race between Senator Niceguy and Robert Goodchance. This case was chosen as the clearest illustration of the courtship stages through the campaign. In chapter 3 the impact of the producer is clearly demonstrated. Not only is the candidate's history important, but so is the history of the state. Local political culture dictates whether or not some self-presentations are acceptable. Producers who come into a race as outsiders and don't do their homework can seriously hurt good candidates. When the "outsider" effect is further complicated by a situation in which one candidate is loaded down with the baggage of the national party, defeat may well be inevitable. In chapter 3 we see how all the elements of a successful courtship are blended in a campaign.

Chapter 4 focuses on the race between Harold Doright and Johnny Fasttrack. Having laid out the stages of the courtship campaign, we begin to focus in more depth on the components of videostyle. This chapter examines the role of the information factor in the courtship campaign. The analysis of this race centers on the importance of the candidate's "history" and the necessity for building on one's previous political base. The nature of the political climate in 1982 may very well have had an impact on the elements of each candidate's videostyle. Chapter 4 traces the campaign history of an incumbent and suggests that incumbent advantage may in part reflect differences in campaign behavior in addition to the greater resources of office. The principal campaign difference between incumbents and challengers is the ease with which incumbents usually control the political agenda—and the consequences when that control is wrested away by the challenger. In chapter 4 we focus in more depth on the importance of what is described in chapter 2 as the "information factor."

Chapter 5 holds constant the effect of outside producers by examining a race where both candidates used local media producers and consultants. The race between Senator Cloistered and Thomas Popular nicely demonstrates how producers who are aware of the political culture and the candidate's history can turn vulnerabilities into safety. The issue of whether candidates or their producers should/do control the candidate's image is again raised. The clash between different philosophies of how the voter decides and what voters look for highlights the general point that nothing is more important than having a candidate who knows why he is running. In chapter 5 we focus in more depth on what has been termed the "intimacy factor."

Chapter 6 reexamines these races and raises again the issue of whether or not they represent the wider universe of campaigns. Although each campaign has its own political nuances which make it unique, each also shares a number of common features. Chapter 6 teases out the commonalities and speculates about "turning points" in the interactions between the candidates and between the candidates and their advisors which might have changed the outcomes of the races.

2

The Campaign as a Courtship

A number of political writers have drawn the analogy between the campaign and a horse race (see, for example, Christopher Arterton's *Media Politics*). Reporters, in particular, have fallen victim to the image and rely on racing terms to convey their analyses. They chronicle the political process from "out of the starting gates" to "neck and neck in the polls" and "winning by a nose." Although useful for some purposes, the horse race metaphor is strained for several reasons.[1]

First, the horse race metaphor implicitly (and often explicitly) makes voters spectators in the political process. In fact, voters are hardly spectators in the electoral process. Second, horse race outcomes are rarely, if ever, measured against expectations. Campaign performance, on the other hand, is often weighed against the expectations of the press, the pollsters and political experts, and of course, the public.[2]

A better understanding of campaigns can be obtained if one views the process as a courtship. A courtship implies action and reaction between all concerned parties. In terms of elections, the courtship campaign may well be democra-

cy's safeguard against political fatigue (on the part of voters).
It is the artful coaxing from the candidates that stimulates
interest and involvement in the mass public. Of course, expectations play a prominent role in the success or failure of
a romance. The ways in which candidates woo their constituents, the manner in which this cozening has adjusted
itself to the changing political environment and the mass
media, are considered here.

The social-psychological research on interpersonal attraction provides a model of the stages of relationships which
can also serve to describe the courtship campaign.[3] There
are five stages of the relationship between candidate and
constituents—initial attraction, building a relationship, continuation, deterioration, and ending. Not every campaign
experiences each phase, just as not all courtships end in
marriage, nor all marriages in divorce.

Initial attraction is sparked by candidates' introductions
to the electorate. Acquaintanceship is the period during
which cognitive barriers to election are overcome. To para-
phrase an old cliché—"to love him, they must know him."

Potential supporters must be aware of the candidates *in
terms of characteristics the supporters deem important*. Initial attraction reflects candidate viability. Advertising that
has a cognitive intent attempts to distinguish candidates
from their opponents. The strategy is to give the candidates
"cue value." "Cue value" is what makes one candidate different or distinguishable from another. The information content of political spots varies, depending on the candidates'
and producers' views of what cues the electorate is seeking.
Cue value may be derived from specific issue positions, ideology, partisanship, group identifications, or personal qualities of the candidate. For cognitive intent to be realized, it is
essential that viewers learn to *recognize* candidate names.
Recognition of the candidate's name on the ballot is the bare

minimum cognitive requirement of a voter for initial attraction to be sparked, and the relationship process to be set in motion.[4]

Once the candidates have become acquainted with their potential constituencies, and voters are aware of them, there is a period of deepening intimacy. This is the time during which candidates attempt to outshine all other suitors, winning trust, and accompanying political loyalty for themselves.

The basic threats to the relationship between candidates and electorate include: 1) too many areas of dissimilarity (role expectations, values, behavior, interests); 2) boredom; 3) changes in reciprocal evaluations; 4) the presence of more desirable alternatives; and 5) perceptions of inequity in commitment, responsibility, or reward.[5]

There is a critical difference between the courtships referred to in social-psychology studies and the courtship that occurs between candidates and constituents. Despite the advent of video dating services (and television's Love Connection), most of the former are still conducted interpersonally. Campaigns, in contrast, are increasingly waged through the mass media. Indeed, television has changed the way candidates campaign. Videostyle is the presentation of self through televised advertising. It encompasses what is said (the verbal message), what is shown (the visual message), and how it is presented (production techniques).[6]

The *presentation of self* is a concept developed by Goffman to describe the process of communication in everyday life. Goffman uses the imagery of the theater to illustrate the struggle between a "performer" to control the expressions given (verbal signs) and the expressions given off (nonverbal signs) and the audience to interpret the meaning of the "performance." The audience accepts and interprets signs, attributing the greatest weight to those which are least explicit—the expressions given off.

The most crucial difference between the interpersonal "information game" Goffman described and political advertising is that the use of television allows candidates to control "the expressions given off." Goffman argued that the " . . . arts of piercing an individual's efforts at calculated unintentionality seem better developed than our capacity to manipulate our own behavior . . . regardless of how many steps have occurred in the information game, the witness is likely to have the advantage over the actor, and the initial asymmetry of the communication process is likely to be retained."[7]

"Goffman did not envision the capacity to edit messages so finely that a presentation can be perfected and polished, controlled and rehearsed, timed and staged. In fact, television advertising supplies candidates with a communications channel through which their nonverbal (and more believable) behavior can be controlled. In television advertising, the candidates can present their messages over and over again until they get it right."[8] Thus, the communication process may still be asymmetrical, but the actor—not the witness—holds the advantage.

It is the presentation of self that creates candidate image. Political commercials permit the candidates to present themselves under the most favorable, highly controlled conditions. The image created is not necessarily false, but it is not necessarily true either. A projected image, by definition, has no depth. Its superficiality need not mean that it is useless. In fact, the truth of the message may be not so much in the factual accuracy of the words and pictures, but in what those words and pictures evoke.[9]

The presentation of self may cause the viewer to think, to feel, or to act: in social-psychological terms, it has cognitive, affective, and/or behavioral consequences. The cognitive dimension reflects candidate viability. If the intended response to the ad is cognitive, the commercial may seek to create or resolve ambiguity, enlarge the viewer's belief system, or create conditions conducive to value clarification. It may elevate certain issues or candidate qualities on the viewer's decisional agenda.[10] The importance of the cognitive dimension is perhaps most clearly stated in the Stokes and Miller axiom, "in order to be perceived favorably, a candidate must first be perceived."[11]

If the intended response to the ad is affective, an emotional response is sought. The affective commercial encourages acceptance or rejection of a candidate. Desensitization, fear, anxiety, shifts in morale or alienation are all affective responses. So too are empathy, identification, trust, excitement, and love.

Behavioral strategies can seek to activate or deactivate the viewer, to encourage the viewer to overtly and publicly express political support (or rejection). Because it is usually difficult to measure what people think or feel (or what they don't do), most of voting research has focused on what they do. But actions are only one side of the behavioral coin. Sometimes the behavioral intent of the ad is deactivation of the opponent's supporters.

The cognitive, affective, and behavioral intentions of the political commercials reflect in some measure the candidates' and producers' views of the mass public and of how the public makes decisions. Candidates must be perceived, they must be liked (supported), and those sentiments must result in a specific behavior at a specific point in time.

The stages of the relationship candidates experience with their constituents are marked by different hurdles. Distinct advertising strategies are more, or less, appropriate at different stages. For example, initial attraction may demand a high level of candidate awareness/recognition.[12] The most successful strategy at this stage may be cognitive. While the voter/viewer is becoming acquainted with the candidate, information about the candidate's education, employment, and other facts may be particularly relevant.

Once the candidates have become acquainted with their potential constituencies, and constituents are aware of them, there is a period of wooing. This is the time during which they attempt to outshine all other suitors, winning the voters' trust, and accompanying political loyalty, for themselves. At this stage, cognitive strategies increasing information about their previous work experience, age, and issue positions are unlikely to win much support. Such information is superficial, and not very useful to the viewer/voter attempting to know them "as a man." At this stage, the critical element in achieving political success is the establishment of an intimate connection with potential supporters. This calls for an affective strategy. Do they share their constituents' values? What promise does the relationship hold for the future? These are the conscious and unconscious questions that the viewer/voter is answering in deciding to whom they will give their hearts and votes. The candidates cannot successfully achieve intimacy without answering them.

The final stage is that at which the relationship is consummated, in other words, support is given to the candidate, the choice of suitors is made. The incumbent and the challenger approach this stage with quite different advantages. The challenger may hold the glamor and excitement of being something new, someone different. This can attract supporters bored or disaffected with the status quo. On the other hand, if presented in the wrong context, being new can mean that the challenger faces greater difficulties. Does his newness connote that the relationship will be a highly risky one? Can he really be depended upon? Is he so new and different that he won't share the values of his state?

The incumbent approaches the situation as the "suitor next door." In place of surprises he offers security. His difficulties arise less from the need to establish identification than from the need to demonstrate that he has not taken the relationship for granted, that he has not moved, psychologically, from his constituents—regardless of how much time he has spent away from them. For the incumbent, the critical factor in retaining support is keeping the romance in the marriage alive. This can be done through attentiveness to his constituents and through showing his deep understanding of them. Such understanding can only come with time. While the novelty of the relationship has worn off, the incumbent has established a deeper intimacy with his constituents. They are partners who respect and can depend upon one another without fail.

From interviews with the candidates and producers, two dimensions were identified as critical to the campaign. The first, an "information factor," has to do with the sources of information that voters rely on and their capacity to absorb that information. The information factor is the sum of many things. It consists not just of issue positions but also of public values. *All* of the candidates were concerned with educating their constituencies. In the cases of the candidates who were unsuccessful, the predominant sentiment seemed to be that if only they could have better informed the voters, the outcome would have been different.

Candidates' concerns with information seem to be greatly influenced by how they view the process of candidate evaluation. Incumbents and challengers see the role of information in the campaign somewhat differently. For the challenger, it is information that produces candidate recognition, that lends cue value to the candidate, and that makes a candidacy viable. For the incumbent, it is information that makes him *vulnerable*. In the six years of a Senate term, the incumbent will inevitably have cast some votes, made some decisions, or failed to respond to some requests that will antagonize part of the constituency. The record itself may be less important than the challenge to explain it. Once that challenge has been seriously issued, by the opponent or the press, the incumbent faces the arduous task of educating constituents. It is information that makes him vulnerable. It is explanation that makes him safe. The greatest threat to the incumbent senator is that he is "teaching" in a classroom of habitually inattentive students, who are likely to pay attention to his challenger at the most inopportune time.[13]

The second critical factor identified in interviews with producers and candidates is the "intimacy factor." Intimacy refers to how comfortable constituents (or potential constituents) feel with the candidate. Intimacy develops on the basis of physical attractiveness, similarity and "reciprocity." It also reflects many other variables. It is a public's judgments about the character of a candidate set against the standards of local political culture. To establish an intimate connection with voters the candidate must engineer a presentation of self that makes voters confident they know the essential nature of his character.[14] It requires a self-presentation that seems to give viewers a glimpse of the soul.

Again, challengers and incumbents can be expected to view intimacy differently. For challengers, putting the voters at ease requires alleviating the fear of the unknown. For the incumbent, continued intimate connection hinges on being reconnected with the state on an emotional and psychological level. Washington—of choice or necessity—will distance the incumbent from his constituents. In each of the races studied here, the distance from Washington to home was great enough to prevent trips there from becoming weekly events. Making voters comfortable with the candidate is a dual task. The voter must feel at ease with the candidate in the familiar home setting but also confident of the candidate's ability to acquit himself well in Washington. For the challenger, establishing a comfortable at-home image may be simpler than reassuring voters about his as yet untested, untried, future behavior should he be elected. For the incumbent, reestablishing his home connection, demonstrating that he has not forgotten his roots, may be more difficult than reassuring voters that he will continue the job along the lines he has already begun to pursue.

The information factor and the intimacy factor play a role in each of the elements of videostyle. Cognitive or affective strategies may be used to communicate information or stimulate intimate connection. Both factors are emphasized by all of the candidates and producers, although to different degrees. The philosophies of the individuals involved, together with their political situations, influence the degree to which the information factor or the intimacy factor are deemed crucial.

The information factor and intimacy factor are discussed explicitly by candidates and producers, and the use of cognitive and affective strategies to build these elements into the media campaign are also explicit. However, none of the candidates or producers stresses the behavioral hurdle in their discussions of their races. This may seem ironic in that the whole point of the campaign is to motivate a specific behavior at a specific time. One reason that the behavioral hurdle may not have been explicitly discussed is that it is better crossed through mediums other than television. There is a danger in using television in a "get out the vote" campaign. That is, a heavy mobilization attempt may scare the opposition into a strong counter-mobilization effort. On the other hand, devices such as phone banks, to call identified supporters, have the desired effect of mobilizing supporters without tipping off the opposition. Furthermore, the candidate wants to make his own supporters aware of the necessity for turning out to vote, without mobilizing their opposition. Because of the inadvertent nature of the commercial audience, television does not allow sufficient discretion in targeting these messages. Direct mail, phone banks, or grass roots organization are better suited to these goals.

As noted earlier, the political situation dictates, in part, the necessity for emphasizing information or emotional connection. In early stages of the campaign, a candidate who is new to politics—for example, running his first statewide race—will be forced to rely on a cognitive strategy. Support will not be widespread until the candidate is well known. However, to know him is not necessarily to like him. Incumbents, or candidates who are well known in their states because of previous public service or other campaigns, have less need to seek pure recognition. Their cognitive strategies are more likely to center on increasing the candidate's cue value.

Affective strategies are extremely common and used throughout the campaign. If the truth of the ad is in the feelings evoked, then all commercials, to some extent, must evoke emotions. In most cases, even the predominantly cognitive spot will contain some affective elements. For the challenger, affective strategies will center on persuading voters to move away from the incumbent (the known) toward the unknown. Raising uncertainty about the incumbent, or negative feelings toward the incumbent, is as important as providing reassurance about the challenger's own course of action once elected. For the incumbent, providing reassurance about his connection with the state and its people is as important as explaining his record.

Situations that encourage the use of affective strategies include those where the incumbent is well known but perhaps only vaguely liked, or those where attitudes toward either candidate are neutral. In these situations, a challenger may use an affective strategy to bring out negative aspects of the incumbent's record. Or, the incumbent, in order to set up a positive field, may use an affective strategy to increase feelings of warmth toward himself. Affective strategies can change perceptions of a candidacy from outer-focused (centered on national issues) to inner-focused (centered on a local/regional agenda).

Because of the demands of being a candidate, an ad campaign cannot reflect the candidate's philosophy exclusively. Time constraints virtually assure that the producer's views will be reflected in the ad as well. However, in the competition between producer and candidate, it is the candidate who ultimately determines what the ingredients of his videostyle will be. Producers can and do generate ideas. They put the ads together and may have a great deal of influence in putting something into, or keeping something out of, the ad campaign. In the races analyzed here, the candidates, with one exception, viewed the final product and gave final approval. When there was something in the ads that they were uncomfortable with, the producer was asked to change it. In one case, ads were completely rejected and returned to the producer. Based on the cases described here, we hypothesize that producers will have the greatest leeway in campaigns devoid of strategic shifts. Incumbents are also hypothesized to relinquish more control over their videostyles than do challengers because of the greater demands of holding office while campaigning.

Candidates do not always seek out producers with philosophies compatible with their own. Nor are they necessarily even aware of the differences. However, candidates who do not think voters can easily absorb issue information are not inclined to use issues in developing a presentation of self. Candidates who recognize their own lack of personal appeal or those who place great faith in the voters' ability to make judgments based on the issues are more likely to use issue information in their presentations of self.

The ultimate success or failure of the campaign can reinforce or alter the importance of information or intimacy in the eyes of candidates and producers. In reflecting about his loss, Thomas Popular (challenger to Senator Cloistered) expressed how running an unsuccessful race on personal appeal had forced him to acknowledge the existence of an issue-based information factor.

> What does he really have to offer in Washington? That's a good question, one we didn't answer. I think they thought that I didn't have enough whiskers—you know, my relative youth and my style as a conciliator rather than a yeller may have given my image a certain softness. The issues just didn't cut that deep. Senator Cloistered had a simple message—stay the course. I didn't have an equitable simple message.
>
> [If I had the race to run over again] I would have been clearer on my opposition to the president and to Senator Cloistered. It was a mistake to try to beguile the voters with my personality and slip through the cracks. We wouldn't have the convoluted strategy we started with. I'll never run a race again on personality. I don't think you can win that way.

Intimacy or information, the views expressed by the candidates and producers are affected by their experiences. Success tends to reinforce a candidate's philosophy, while defeat tends to challenge it.[15] Videostyles are flexible, evolving with the candidate even after one race. The presentation of self in one campaign will be altered in the next, as the first experience is incorporated into the candidate's vision of himself and his job.

In summary, what is videostyle? Videostyle is the way that candidates present themselves to voters through television advertising. The intimacy factor and the information factor are components of videostyle critical to the presentation of self. They are expressed through the verbal, nonverbal, and production content of the commercial. The campaign process itself is a courtship. Videostyles are shaped by the political situations candidates find themselves in, the context of their races, and the philosophies of the candidates and producers. The spots used to present the candidates have cognitive, affective, and occasionally behavioral intentions. At different stages of the courtship, different strategies are appropriate. The use of a cognitive or affective strategy to evoke certain feelings hinges on the relative importance that candidates and producers place on cognition and affect in their theories of how voters decide.

3

Good Senators Wear White Hats

Just what are we, the governed, doing when we choose between two candidates in the modern media campaign? Since the late 1940s scholars have been seeking to explain voting behavior through large-scale quantitative studies of elections.[1] The questions of how voters decide and what elections mean have held particular significance for researchers since the answers to these questions reflect on the extent to which one can call our form of government "democratic." The ways in which scholars have pursued this line of research have had enormous and sometimes serendipitous consequences.[2]

Practitioners of politics are often criticized for marketing candidates like soap or cake mix or some other consumable product.[3] In fact, an early interest of Paul Lazersfeld, one of the fathers of electoral research, was consumer decisions. Frustrated in attempting to unravel complex processes such as how career choices are made, he turned to the study of consumer preferences, radio program popularity, etc., in order to begin to understand basic cognitive and decision processes. Prior to the 1940 presidential election, Lazersfeld proposed to study the election using a consumer panel design relating media exposure to vote choice.[4] Lazersfeld had been unable to obtain funding to study changes in brand preference and advertising, and the presidential campaign was considered an analogous process. This project, with a less commercial focus and obvious importance, won the financial support of the Rockefeller Foundation and Time, Inc. That candidates' campaigns may resemble product marketing, skeletally, has been widely noted. That social scientists have intellectual roots in market research techniques is less widely known. However, those ties have influenced the way in which the electoral process and voter decision making have been conceptualized and explained.

Social scientists have focused on the voter (consumer) and time of decision (purchase dynamics). Party identification parallels brand loyalty. The candidates are scrutinized side by side as if they were two products on the same shelf. In contrast, the courtship perspective presented here acknowledges that, indeed, the candidates may not be running the same race at all.[5]

This chapter provides an in-depth, qualitative look at television campaigning using a courtship perspective. The courtship perspective focuses attention on the development and maintenance of a relationship between the public and the elected official.

One of the most important consequences of candidates' increasing reliance on television to communicate their messages is that the messages must now be translated by a producer. The flow of communication between candidate and constituent is no longer direct—as it is in the interpersonal setting. The political commercial reflects *candidates' and producers'* philosophies of how voters decide. Thus, the choices that voters make—to the extent that these choices are influenced by political advertising—are choices between two producers as well as two candidates. Political producers may not be accountable to the public in the same ways, or to the same extent, that elected representatives are. How much influence are producers having on the political process? How do candidates go about building a relationship with voters? What, indeed, are we doing when we choose between two candidates in the modern media campaign?

To Court or Not to Court

Like a relationship, a campaign has a beginning. The candidates see an opportunity and decide to run. Jacobson and Kernell (1983) have analyzed the strategic importance of this phase of the campaign. Bernstein (1977) has looked at the impact of the primary contest.[6] Politicians weigh the probability of winning based on the political climate and other strategic considerations before committing themselves. A highly competitive primary situation, for example, has been linked to a lower probability of winning in the general election. More generally, the beginnings of a campaign in terms of the decision to run and competitiveness of the nomination process have been explicitly linked to outcomes.

This is the beginning of a U.S. Senate race in Magic State. In the particular case at hand, probable contenders were defined quite early, and neither faced a divisive primary. Magic State has a tradition of split-ticket voting, although it tends to favor the Republicans in terms of voter registration. Third party candidates have done well historically, and the state was one of the first to grant women the right to vote. The party organizations are weak, and campaigns tend to be run on a personal basis. Magic State experienced rapid growth, particularly in the 1970s, but the growth has left intact the rugged individualist spirit that in the past nurtured split-ticket voting. The basis for about half of the employment in the state is the exploitation of the state's wealth of natural resources.

Senator Matthew Niceguy's earliest campaign was based on establishing a strong identification with the state. He is fiercely independent, moderate to conservative, with a warm expansiveness that embodies the spirit of Magic State. Matthew Niceguy doesn't look like the stereotypical U.S. senator. He looks like Magic State—a mountain of a man, more comfortable in blue jeans than blue suit, more in awe of the powerful Magic landscape than the aura of power to be found in Washington. Matt has a warm ready smile that exudes sincerity and concern. Perhaps these qualities, combined with his formidable campaign skills, are the key to his political success. Matt Niceguy has the reputation for being the nicest person in the U.S. Senate. According to a key campaign aide and administrative assistant:

> As part of our strategy we had to look at the possibility of running against the governor [CatnMouse]. One of our strategies was to raise a significant amount of money early and make no secret of it to discourage the top tier opposition. We started raising money in 1980. By mid-year 1981 we wanted to have a lot so all the world would see he was dead set on winning it. In our hearts we always thought we'd run against Goodchance. The governor is an older man. His family is well taken care of in the governor's mansion. He has a higher salary. Our ploy was to make sure people knew it was a tough race so they would contribute. Of the one million [dollars] raised, nearly half came from Magic State.[7]

Robert Goodchance, the challenger, has been a top vote getter in his races for the state legislature and, prior to his 1982 bid for a U.S. Senate seat, was seen by many as the brightest hope of the Democratic party in Magic State. He began campaigning for the U.S. Senate a year before the election in an effort to get his name known statewide. Bob is young, a native of Magic State, and somewhat more liberal than Matt Niceguy. He gathered endorsements from a number of liberal groups, including organized labor. While in the state legislature, Bob worked hard for increased funding for education, and health and environmental issues, and led the battle over ratification of the Equal Rights Amendment to the United States Constitution in Magic State.

When Bob Goodchance and Matt Niceguy served in the state legislature together, they had been close on a number of issues—mental health, child welfare. In Bob's own words:

> I saw him as a Charles Percy progressive Republican. But in Washington he went through a transformation, becoming a Jesse Helms conservative. Constituent groups who had supported him were disappointed. My decision [to run] was based on him, not Reagan and the Republican conservatives. . . .
>
> We had problems in that the Democratic Senate Campaign Committee wanted Governor CatnMouse to run for Senate. They thought he could win. The governor said privately that he wouldn't, but refused to say it publicly. So we had a long time without the support of the national campaign committee, when people were waiting to see what would happen.

Thus, the stage was set for the general election. The incumbent began two years before the race to shape the environment in which he would run. This largely consisted of presenting a strong posture for all the world to see of financial clout and personal popularity. The challenger devoted his attentions during this period to persuading others that he would indeed be the standard bearer and was the credible alternative to the incumbent.

Initial Attraction: Physical and Personality Appeal

"Initial attraction" is the first hurdle a challenger must overcome in seeking office. Candidates' first presentations of themselves are designed to spark initial attraction and interest. Part of being perceived as a credible candidate is generating favorable first impressions. What is important in these first impressions? How do relationships between candidates and voters evolve from them?

Social psychologists have established that relationships develop between people on the basis of physical attractiveness, similarity, and reciprocity of evaluations.[8] For example, research shows that women respond positively to men having thin legs, a thin waist, broad shoulders, small buttocks, and being of tall or medium height.[9] Men, on the other hand, are attracted to women with medium-sized breasts, legs, and buttocks.[10]

Some research has demonstrated that physically attractive individuals benefit by being perceived as poised, interesting, sociable, independent, exciting, and sexually warm. Attractive individuals are also perceived as more masculine or feminine.[11]

In addition, certain personality characteristics are perceived as more attractive than others. Smiling, expressiveness, and outgoingness are perceived as attractive in males, and dominant individuals of either gender are preferred to relatively submissive ones. Competitive individuals are perceived as more attractive, and disclosing strangers are preferred to those unwilling to reveal much.[12]

A number of voting studies have demonstrated that voters are highly performance oriented in their assessments of candidate image. Thus, physical attractiveness is hypothesized to be important 1) when candidates are difficult to differentiate, 2) very early in the campaign before performance relevant information becomes widely known, and 3) among extremely unsophisticated voters.

Political scientists, as a rule, have not devoted much time or effort to identifying the characteristics of the physically attractive candidate. We can speculate, however, that the

vision people hold of the ideal lover varies from the vision
they hold of the ideal senator. Moreover, just as there is variation among people in their assessments of date attractiveness, there is probably variation among people in their
assessments of candidate attractiveness. One recent study
demonstrates the importance of physical appearance in de-
termining how people vote.[13]

The importance of initial attraction in the context of
Magic State underlies the challenger's perceptions of how
voters are evaluating him. Physical attractiveness is not explicitly mentioned by the candidate, however some aspects
of personality attractiveness are referred to.

> Around here it's a real personal thing. They evaluate you on a
> personal level, as opposed to making the decision on the is-
> sues only. Do you appear to be honest, sincere, too slick, too
> much a politician? They evaluate you as they do neighbors
> and friends. The issues are important only as they relate to
> that. They can accept a disagreement on the issues if they
> like you. The charge that I was too liberal stuck because of
> my age, because of my association with the Ted Kennedy
> camp in 1980. On gun control, my association with Kennedy
> overrode my own position on the issue. On the other is-
> sues—tax breaks and social security—it became a credibility
> issue. People here [in Hometown] thought I was hardworking
> and represented the people. I had no problems with my credi-
> bility in [Hometown.]

> [I think people saw me as] hardworking. I said that before,
> and that was part of the strategy. I believed Niceguy to be a
> lazy senator. Part of the strategy was to work hard to demon-
> strate that. On the negative side, I think it did come down to
> a credibility thing. The other thing Niceguy did was in radio
> commercials. He said, "Goodchance is a young, ambitious
> lawyer who would say anything to get elected." People here
> don't like that. They don't trust lawyers, or ambition, when
> it's put that way.

Initial Attraction: Similarity

We tend to like those whom we perceive as similar to us because it validates our own judgments about the world. A certain balance is achieved when two people like each other equally.[14] (Similarity can be expressed verbally or nonverbally.) Not only do we like those we perceive as similar to us, but we perceive those we like as agreeing with us. Issues and personality information are important insofar as they demonstrate similarity. Similarity can be heightened through agreement on issues, physical appearance, or setting. By dressing as his constituents do, and showing himself in familiar settings, the candidate demonstrates visually that he is like them, one of them. Similarity is important in building the relationship—providing a transition from acquaintance to intimacy. Deterioration can occur when any of these elements—physical attractiveness, similarity, or reciprocity—are absent or miscommunicated.

If the distinction between appealing physical and personality traits seems somewhat blurred, there is a reason. Psychologists have found that there is a tendency for people to select partners similar to themselves.[15] Moreover, couples who are not similar are more likely to break up. Other research demonstrates that it is possible to predict with reasonable accuracy how much one person will like another on the basis of the proportion of similar attitudes they hold.[16] The implications of these findings in the political context are: 1) candidates who hold attitudes or values that are very different from those of their constituents are less likely to be elected and, if elected, more likely to be defeated in successive elections; 2) issues are an obvious opportunity for challengers to establish similarity with potential constituents. For the challenger in Magic State, Bob Goodchance, similarity is an obstacle because his own issue values are overridden by his association with the national Democratic party's issue positions.

> [In terms of issues] I think people associated me with environmental issues, wilderness, arms control—and thought I'd do a better job than Niceguy. They saw Matt doing a better job on economic issues. I had trouble in the campaign with what my party was doing nationally. A lot of the problem I had was created by the baggage of the national party image. That was one of the key problems—this thing of Reagan needing a Republican Senate to continue [his program]. People weren't convinced the Democrats would do any better.

Initial Attraction: Reciprocity

Our attraction to others is heavily influenced by others' perceptions of us. Positive interactions such as eye contact, leaning forward, engaging in conversation, and propinquity lead to acquaintanceship. Acquaintance becomes familiarity and friendship through verbal and nonverbal signs of mutual respect, interest, and affection. Reciprocity is important because we expect the words and actions of others to match our feelings toward them. When these expectations are not met, attraction can change dramatically.[17] Reciprocity is crucial to maintaining initial attraction and continuing the relationship.

In the political context, reciprocity may be important for incumbents and challengers in different ways. Particularly for the challenger, reciprocity may take the form of future promises. While the challenger can certainly return the goodwill and affection of potential constituents, he is not in a position to do anything for them yet. Still, he asks them for support so that in the future he can provide jobs, government projects, and other benefits.

For the incumbent, reciprocity is important as well. The discussion, however, will center on what has been done in the past as well as what is promised for the future. In the case of Magic State, the clearest example of communication of reciprocity occurs in a spot produced for the incumbent. This spot stresses reciprocity of evaluations. Constituents are shown that the incumbent knows them as intimately as they know him.

The political ad in question features Matt Niceguy talking about Magic State. The spot is quiet and reflective. We see a silhouette of Matt putting on his cowboy hat and opening the door of his home. He stands, poised, a shadow against the bright Magic State sunshine. The sunlight streams in the door. The mountains, trees, and a white fence are brought into focus through the open door. Matt walks out. The camera pans the mountains in the background and valley in the foreground. The camera cuts to a small diner. It is clearly the local gathering place. Men and women are sitting at the counter, and Matt enters, greeting them individually. A waitress pours coffee. Matt shakes hands, smiling broadly, tips his hat to a lady. He is smiling and talking, greeting friends and neighbors. Always the same broad grin, the dimples punctuating his smile. The camera cuts to a shot of Matt standing next to a pick-up truck and talking. Again, the dominant feature of the shot is the warm expansive smile. The spot ends with a shot of Matt walking across a field.

Throughout the spot, Matt is dressed in blue jeans, plaid shirt, down vest, and cowboy hat. He looks like Magic State—rugged, imposing, strong of character, at once both tough and warm. Above the low croon of a harmonica we hear him talk about the place he represents, the people. His voice is reflective, the words filled with deep respect and affection. Despite his comment that "I am Magic State," there is not a trace of conceit.

To somebody that's never seen Magic State, I can describe it as a place that's almost magical in its dimensions. First, and foremost, it's a state full of enormous horizons. Well, Magic State is beautiful. It's got mountains, water, deserts, prairies, and what have you. [Pause.] It's home. It's where I grew up. It's what I am. I am Magic State. It's the very people I represent. The people that love each other, that work hard, that are devout, that are ambitious, that are self-reliant. They believe in this country. And that's Magic State.

In describing his constituency, Matt Niceguy further elaborates on the qualities of the people he represents. His identification with the state is strongly reflected in the mix of healthy respect and affection. In a personal interview Matt Niceguy describes his constituency as

Irascible. And I mean that in tribute really. Magic State has an astonishing ability to ticket-split. Generally, it's conservative but more oriented toward human charity and human issues. You can offend the hell out of them with one issue.

Campaigning, you find a very sophisticated attitude. Going door to door you can't be over-prepared. People will talk to you about foreign aid, foreign trade. I think it's partly because they spend a lot of time alone. They are better read because they are alone and not being entertained.

Tactics of a Challenge

Robert Goodchance hired B. McClure as his media producer. McClure is a free-lance consultant who had worked in a primary campaign and had done some work for candidates in local races in other states previously. At the time of the Magic State race McClure was somewhat new to the business of producing political spots; and this was the first major state-wide race McClure would handle.

According to McClure, an attempt was made to communicate each element—attractiveness (senatorial appearance), reciprocity, and similarity.

> One thing we did while shooting was make him look dignified, experienced, and a little older than he was. In Magic State, TV doesn't reach everywhere. For him to come out punching would have been a mistake. We started out positive.
>
> You want people to look at your candidate as if he is already in the position [the office]. So I tried to make him look senatorial where possible. We had spots with the governor, and with him all dressed up, head-on. The family spot we did because that's important in Magic State.
>
> In voting against an incumbent there is a lot of fear of the unknown. They don't just judge your candidate, you first have to get them to move away from the other candidate. I think people want someone who they see as an office holder. People expect politicians to be almost saintlike.
>
> People want someone hardworking, smart, someone who will make their state look good, look out for their interests. Sometimes that is even at the expense of honesty and trustworthiness, because they don't believe that exists anyway. . . . It's hard to get people to trust someone who's running for public office. . . . He wasn't well known enough [to be associated with issues]. It was sort of like a clean slate. The problem in Magic State, eventually Bob was perceived as one of those knee-jerk eastern liberals who is for everything they're supposed to be for.[18]

The inexperience of the producer reveals itself in the ads produced. McClure was unaccustomed to telling a story visually in thirty to sixty seconds, having worked on documentaries and other longer film segments. Many of the devices used in Goodchance's spots are standard techniques. Yet the elements do not work together as a whole. Only one of the spots successfully evokes the intimacy necessary for effective courting of the electorate. The others lack warmth and create distance. Television is a visual medium. The viewer must be *shown*, not told. When the ads themselves are viewed, the flaws in the execution of strategy become more apparent.

A testimonial spot produced for Robert Goodchance and aired in the early part of the campaign exemplifies the producer's effort to translate the challenger's presentation of self. The spot discussed here is "positive" in that it focuses on people's reasons for supporting the challenger. A negative spot was also aired featuring the same format and most of the same people—this time stating their reasons for opposing the incumbent. On the whole, it is difficult to empathize with the people expressing their reasons for not supporting Senator Niceguy because we know so little about them.

The spot opens with a medium shot of a young woman in a white blouse, short dark brown hair, brown eyes, chubby. She is clearly outdoors—there are trees in the background, and the light is very bright. The camera cuts to a shot of a middle-aged man in the same background. He is dressed in a tan sports coat, white shirt and tie, and he is wearing glasses. Cut again to a shot of a woman standing in front of a window, a building in the background. She is thirtyish, with short brown hair, dressed in a short-sleeved white blouse. Cut again to a shot of a white-haired old woman in a blue suit with white blouse. There is a butterfly pin on the jacket lapel. The camera cuts again to the same young woman in the opening shot, then to the white-haired old woman in the blue suit, then to the thirtyish woman again. Cut to a middle-aged woman with frizzy brown hair streaked with grey, wearing a blue and white print shirt. Cut to an overweight middle-aged man, dressed in a light blue shirt. The final shot is a blue background with white letter graphic display of the slogan "Goodchance, U.S. Senate." A picture of

Goodchance is in the lower right corner. He is dressed in a blue suit, white shirt, and red tie. The oversize frames of his glasses give him an owlish appearance.

All of the movement in the spot is done through camera cuts—the persons are shown looking straight into the camera, standing still. All of the shots are from the chest up. The spot is only thirty seconds, so each individual is shown only briefly as they speak. The audio content is each individual's reason for supporting Goodchance. Perhaps most striking is what is absent from the spot, rather than what is present. All of the individuals featured appear to be white middle-class people; they are predominantly young to middle aged, and predominantly female. There is nothing in their dress or manner to associate them with the locale—they are "generic." In the spots produced for Matt Niceguy, by contrast, the individuals are more easily identified with the state through their dress or manner. This testimonial for Goodchance doesn't tell a story the way the casework spots (discussed later) do for the incumbent. The candidate appears only in a photograph at the very end of the spot for a split second. The pictures are boring; the quick cuts of the camera do little to relieve the sameness of the shots; and the audio content fails to provide the intimate connection with either the endorser or the candidate. In Senator Niceguy's casework spots we get to know the citizens and develop empathy for their problems. This empathy gives us a reason to believe their endorsement of the senator. In Goodchance's testimonial spots we see each citizen too briefly and too superficially for any feeling to be evoked. If the truth of the ad lies in the sentiment evoked, this spot fails because the viewer is never shown the reason lying behind the citizen's endorsement of Goodchance.

Young woman: I believe I would have a voice in Washington with Robert Goodchance as my Senator.

      Man: He's the type of person you can talk to, explain things to, and reason with.

   Woman: He's just like all the rest of us. He'll listen to what we have to say.

   Woman: He has the courage of his convictions.

   Woman: He's had extensive experience.

   Woman: He's hardworking. He's articulate.

   Woman: His interests are with the people of Magic State.

   Woman: I think he will be more responsive to our needs than our current Senator.

      Man: I am very definitely supporting Robert Goodchance.

Announcer: Robert Goodchance for United States Senate.

For a candidate with a fundamental recognition problem, it seems odd to spend precious advertising time on a spot that shows so little of him. The only time the challenger is shown is at the end of the spot in a somewhat unflattering photograph. The use of a photo instead of a live shot of the candidate also creates distance. It heightens the sense of being removed from what is happening on the screen. Although Matt Niceguy also uses stills at the end of his spots, these follow on the heels of segments that have had the camera follow him as he goes about the activities of his daily life—working, meeting people in the state, etc. Thus, the stills provide closure for the intimacy that is aroused. The challenger's spot does not evoke that intimacy. Thus, the impact of the still photo at the end of the spot is quite different.

Three other spots designed to attract supporters were aired by the Goodchance campaign. One has a "jobs" focus, the other is in a formal setting, and the third is the endorsement by the governor of Magic State, Governor CatnMouse. Each is an attempt to show similarity between the challenger's values and the state's values by talking about issues.

The jobs spot opens with a shot of empty railroad cars. The camera is above a trainyard, looking down from a high angle. The camera pans the empty railyard, moves to examine the tracks leading nowhere, and rests on Goodchance, walking beside the railroad cars. He is dressed in tan slacks, white shirt, and dark blue tie. He walks toward the camera. His look is serious, and he is gesturing toward the viewer as he speaks. Goodchance continues walking into a medium shot. He gestures directly at the audience. The camera cuts to a blue background with white graphic letters and a still photo of Goodchance. As these images appear on the screen, we hear Robert Goodchance speak directly to us:

> These cars are empty now. They used to be full of coal and uranium heading for market. But now they just sit. And a lot of people around Magic State, who used to be working, are sitting too. Waiting to be productive again. Now, I know a United States Senator can't work miracles. But one thing you can do is make sure that Magic State's voice is heard loud and clear in Washington, and that's just what I plan to do. I'm Robert Goodchance, and that's why I'm running for the United States Senate.

Instead of surrogates we hear the challenger himself. As it turns out, he has a clear, strong voice. He appears at ease in front of the camera. With shirt sleeves rolled up, he looks relaxed, and more than that—approachable, energetic. The shortcoming of the ad is that the candidate is alone. His connection to the people of Magic State is not explicit. His understanding of the character of Magic State—in order to represent it in a "loud and clear voice"—is similarly vague.

A formal spot also takes advantage of Goodchance's ability to speak directly into the camera, and his strong, dynamic voice. The spot opens with a medium shot of Goodchance (chest and up). He is framed against a black/dark blue background. He is dressed in a dark blue suit, white shirt, and red tie. Again, he wears the oversize glasses which give him an owlish look. He is looking directly into the camera. The camera lingers at a medium shot, then slowly moves in for a close-up of his face at the end. We hear Robert Goodchance speaking directly to us.

> A senator can help bring new jobs and investment to Magic State without sacrificing our clean air and water, hunting and fishing, or the qualities of our schools, communities, and people. We can have a prosperous economy without giving up what we like best about Magic State, if we have a senator who cares enough to work for the proper balance by making sure that our voice is heard, loud and clear, in Washington. I'm Robert Goodchance, and that's why I'm running for the United States Senate.

Again, the shortcoming of this spot is that it offers little of visual interest. Devices construed to give Goodchance the appearance of authority (the formal attire and setting) serve to create distance between him and the viewer. Again, the challenger's connection to the state, and its people, is a hollow one. He is shown alone. Far more stirring would be shots of the challenger talking to people in the state, shirt sleeves rolled up, at work, or even at play, enjoying the "clean air and water, hunting and fishing" and showing some identification with the schools, communities, and people. The message as presented does little to further identification with the challenger. There is no warmth between challenger and audience—no intimate connection.

Building a Relationship

Once the candidates have been introduced to their potential constituencies, and awareness of their presence has been established, there is a period of deepening intimacy. This is followed by an attempt by the candidate to build a relationship on this foundation of awareness. Successful candidates must now outshine all other potential suitors, winning trust and the accompanying political loyalty for themselves. There must be a certain chemistry between candidates and potential constituents. Incumbents and challengers must build relationships in different ways since they begin the relationships from different starting points.[19]

Despite the preponderance of evidence that retrospective evaluations of performances in office carry great weight with voters, the candidates and producers interviewed here are concerned with future promises.[20] In their quest to build a relationship with voters, challengers especially cannot rely on a shared past, nor can they afford to depend on the here and now. What romance reaches its true heights if the attitude of the suitor is "this is it, we have today"? No, that is a liaison more likely to smolder than burn. Yearning is important. Real intimacy stems from the sense that there is a future and it holds something impossibly good and worthwhile. Even if that future is just beyond grasping, even if it requires some sacrifice and delayed gratification, future promises are a potent fuel firing the passions of the electorate. All the candidates must do is *show* the future.

Only one of the spots produced for Goodchance achieves intimate connection between the viewer and the candidate. It is a spot referred to by the producer as the "family spot." This ad is distinctive in that it lets the pictures reveal something of the character of the candidate. The camera follows the movement of the man, rather than creating action through cutting. It also places the candidate in a distinctly Magic State setting. The spot is vividly positive in tone.

The visual portion of the ad begins with a long shot of Goodchance holding his young son's hand as they walk along a mountain path. The father and son are clearly very close.

As he says, "Let's walk right over here" he gestures toward an easier path—unobstructed by fallen logs and tall grass. The camera fades to a shot of a large river or lake, with people in the distance. Slowly the people in the distance are brought into close range. It is Robert Goodchance with his wife and son, and he is teaching the boy to fish. They are practicing casting, one parent on each side of the boy. The camera moves in for a close-up of the young boy reeling in his line. There is a change of camera angles as we see the delight on his face. The camera pauses for a medium shot of Goodchance helping his young son holding the fishing rod steady. Beneath this scene are white letter graphics spelling out the message, "Goodchance for Senate."

This, more than any other spot produced for the challenger, shows the viewer what kind of man Robert Goodchance is. The way the spot is filmed creates a "day in the life of" sensation. The viewer is treated to a glimpse of the man with his family. He is a man who loves the Magic State land, and enjoys its breathtaking beauty. He is a man devoted to his wife and son. All the shots show him either touching, or in very close physical proximity, to both. The voice-over features the words and voice of the challenger, but we don't see him speaking the part. Rather, the sensation is one of being privy to his innermost thoughts and feelings. The candidate comes across as young, yes, but the youth is not translated into inexperience. He looks at ease, not stuffy, idealistic, not ambitious, driven, if at all, by the protective instinct—to shelter and provide for a family. Perhaps most importantly there is a sense of balance. The sterility of many of the other spots is gone, and there is a relaxed quality. The contrast between this "family" spot and the testimonial spot described earlier—is stark.

The audio portion of the family spot spot features Robert Goodchance talking about his involvement in government, and the relation between his public service activities and his family life. The audio content is thus highly personalized. A male announcer simply introduces him:

Announcer: Robert Goodchance.
Goodchance: Let's walk right over here. [Pause.] I've been involved in state government for more than ten years in Magic State. And I've been fascinated with the whole new meaning that my involvement in government has gained because of my concern about my son's future [Pause.] What kind of schools he'll attend [Pause.] Whether or not there'll be jobs [Pause.] The quality of life in Magic State [Pause.] We don't want this to be the last generation of Americans with the opportunity to do better than our parents did.
Announcer: Goodchance for Senate.

The future that is shown here is one of families united to build a better state. Visually and verbally the message is the same. The candidate is in sync with the values of the community. The intimate connection between challenger and voter/viewer snaps into place because the candidate's presentation of self allows the viewer a glimpse of the man— stripped of everything but his reason for running.

This connection between candidate and viewer cannot be established if the level of knowing between them remains merely at the level of awareness. Knowing a name, some unilluminating facts about occupation, education, career, is no basis for a marriage, much less a vote. Even issue information may provide no more than a superficial acquaintanceship.[21] Establishing an intimate connection requires that viewers discover what kind of people the candidates are— and what they promise for the future. These are reasons to elect them.

The incumbents approach the task of building a relationship quite differently from the challengers. In place of surprises they offer security. Should incumbents grow inattentive with the years there are simple and effective ways of regaining their attention. A close election, and the ever present threat of defeat, can keep the romance steaming. Unlike a husband, an incumbent knows that there is always another suitor.

Senator Niceguy also sees the importance of both conveying issue information and putting voters at ease in building a relationship. Issues are not "guiding" but *can* serve to alienate supporters. The campaign is almost a "friends and neighbors" affair. Word of mouth, recognition, establishing integrity and accessibility are keys to winning. According to Matt Niceguy:

> I don't think they're [voters] so issue specific in a general way as you might hope they'd be. *Campaigning comes down to one or two issues and a lot of emotion attached to it.* It's the ability to identify a candidate. TV does nothing but serve as a general introduction to the candidate. People are trying to recognize you. Most of your support comes from word of mouth. TV is very powerful but not all powerful. My guess is it's some integrity and accessibility. Not mirror image integrity. They will tolerate some differences with you, but an acceptable level of integrity.
>
> One of the things we worried most about was how to get come clarity on an issue. I'm not sure we ever achieved that. The single greatest perception was honesty and integrity, but no one issue—we improved on water.
>
> I was taken to task on a lot of issues, but they didn't seem to be guiding. We made a lot of effort, but it didn't seem to be guiding. [Emphasis added.]

The incumbent's presentation of self in the early part of the campaign vividly reevokes his intimate connection with the state. Similarity and reciprocity are communicated in every aspect of his videostyle—from the setting of the spot, to his dress and manner, to the verbal message, to the production techniques. Incumbent and challenger share similar views of how voters decide. Despite their basic underlying philosophical agreement, the translation of their messages by their respective producers leads to distinct videostyles. We have described in great detail the philosophy and tactics of the challenger through initial attraction and building a relationship. Let us now examine more closely the tactics of the incumbent in building his relationship with constituents.

Strategy for an Incumbent

While clearly the candidates themselves have a great deal of influence on the campaign messages presented, the producers are primarily responsible for translating that message on film. Brad Show was brought in from outside Magic State to produce Senator Niceguy's political spots. He is an experienced director, writer, and producer of television advertising. Professionally, he has worked as a journalist and as a press-secretary in a congressional office. Since beginning his work as an advertising producer, he has worked on a number of gubernatorial, senatorial, and congressional campaigns, as well as producing ads for referendum issues and commercial products. In off campaign years, he consults with businesses interested in developing public relations programs. In 1982, he was producing ads for six different campaigns, simultaneously with his work for Senator Niceguy. The extent to which the producer's personal political philosophy reflects itself in the ads is very clear. The ads for Niceguy and Doright in 1982 reveal the same formulae. Brad

Show perceived the same strategic necessity for both clients. In his words:

> For Niceguy an overview [of strategy] would be very similar to Doright [see chapter 4]. Both were regarded as someone who had moved from their constituency, for whatever reason. The strategic necessity was to reconnect them with the state. We did spots that talked about Niceguy's accomplishments . . . Magic State and what he thought of it . . . pictured him in the state, and casework. We used more casework in Magic State because we had better access to cases and less of a need to attack. Cases were beautiful, made to order—and countered the opponent's arguments. There was a heavy preponderance of cases on social security, on railroad retirement or pension. There was a child custody case that had a high profile in the state and worked very well. We were also able to use Reagan—Magic State is largely Republican. Reagan cut a spot for Niceguy also.
>
> Goodchance was in the state legislature and, I think it was in 1980, he missed more days than anyone else in the legislature. He had also served as Ted Kennedy's campaign manager in the state. That knowledge got disseminated through direct mail. Magic State is a small state. More people work in the World Trade Center than in the entire state.
>
> Targeting was easy in Magic State. In that state all you have to do is bring home the Republicans. There are some conservative Democrats. Some issues that can hurt you if you're not careful—eastern Republicans tend to be staunch environmentalists.
>
> We went on the air when Niceguy announced. He announced late. In May we did three spots: "accomplishments," "Niceguy on Magic State" (the good guy stuff) and the "reassurance" spot may have been in there, though that was less of a need. In late August and September we did specific issues. They ran on radio first; some casework spots, and an environmental and agriculture spot on radio. In mid-October for ten days to two weeks we did the attack spots. The Sena-

tor Lincoln spot ran longer [endorsement by another U.S. senator]. Then we ended with the "good guy" spots and added the Reagan endorsement.[22]

For Brad Show, the purpose of the campaign was to reconnect the incumbent with his constituents. The incumbent's qualities which were attractive to voters in the previous campaign had to be reevoked. Doubts about candidate-constituency similarity had to be laid to rest.

Senator Niceguy relied heavily on *local* advisors for the development of strategy and checking the communication of spots. These other advisors of Matt Niceguy (an administrative assistant and the former campaign manager) demonstrated a deeper understanding of, and sensitivity to, local political culture. The administrative aide, Joe Gallup, outlines the strategy used going into the campaign.

> We tried to keep Matt above the fray. We were in a strong position with a strong incumbent but we recognized we were running in a bad year. Bob Goodchance was perceived as the brightest hope of the Democratic party, except maybe for the governor. He was in the state legislature and associated with a former congressman as far back as law school. He had a good reputation as electable in his home county. Goodchance did something unusual in Magic State. He ran as a declared candidate beginning in 1981, for a total of fourteen months. He raised a good deal of money—when all was said and done he spent $600,000. As it stands now, the only one who spent more is Matt (about one and a half million).

The former campaign manager, Brian Windy, is primarily concerned with protecting potential vulnerabilities of the senator and distancing the incumbent from his challenger, as a means of reducing the credibility of the challenger.

> What was lacking was any strong issue *anchor* although his issue record was strong. It wasn't in place. It gave our opposition a foothold, because of a lack of strong issue identity,

to paint it. It was a race to give Matt his issue identity before the opposition could paint it.

As long as we could, we ran an issue-oriented campaign. Tried to hammer his record and ignore the opponent. He [Matt] was never put in the position of answering his opponent directly. It wasn't until the last three weeks that Matt answered Goodchance directly and that was in response to erroneous charges.

[The senator's natural constituency] is mainstream Republican support, the agricultural community, the [widget] industry. They are responsible for nearly half of all employment in Magic State, and this may have backfired on Goodchance. He was running around saying that Matt represented the [widget] industry.

When the senator was elected in 1976 he was perceived as a maverick and liberal and he didn't have mainstream Republican support. Postelection surveys showed Matt carried a high percentage of the environmental vote. The environmental leadership seemed to be out of step with their own community.

Achieving Intimate Reconnection

As Brad Show stated, the ads produced in the first wave of media included an "accomplishments" spot, a "reassurance," spot, and one he called "Niceguy on Magic State." The "Matt on Magic State" ad has already been described in detail. Thus, we shall turn to an examination of the other two spots. Each of these spots was critical because they set the context for all the other campaign information which the voter/viewer was to receive. "Setting up a positive field" or "painting an identity" is a strategy that assumes that it is easier to help people form initial opinions than to change an opinion already formed.[23] Coming in early in the campaign with positive information is a part of each of the candidate's strategies discussed in this book, although executed with varying degrees of success.

The accomplishments spot for Matt Niceguy has more visual impact than the spot produced by Brad Show for Hal Doright (chapter 4), though the audio content is virtually identical.[24] It is only thirty seconds long. However, the preponderance of shots which include Matt Niceguy show him dressed casually—not in his senatorial blue suit, but in his blue jeans. This is clearly a departure from what has become de rigour dress in senatorial ads and subtly, but effectively, makes the point that Matt is one of "us"—not one of "them." There are, of course, a few shots that show Matt in Washington—precisely, three. One shows him seated in a committee hearing. A transition shot shows him walking down a hallway with two staffers; and the third shows him at his desk writing.

The spot begins with a shot of Matt, dressed in jeans, down vest, and cowboy hat walking down the main street of any town in Magic State. He is smiling, shaking hands and greeting people. The camera cuts to a shot of him seated in a committee hearing with a graphic bullet about legislation he worked on. The camera cuts to a shot of Matt walking down the Senate hallway with two staffers. Then cuts again to a shot of the Magic State outdoors. Cut to a shot of Matt walking across a field, smiling (somewhat shyly this time), again dressed in red plaid shirt, blue jeans, down vest, and cowboy hat. The camera lingers on him as he moves forward, cutting away at the point where he has walked into a close-up shot. He is seated at his desk, writing, coat off, tie loosened, American flag in the background. His brow is furrowed in thought. The camera cuts again quickly to a shot of him in a sporting goods store (fishing rod in the background), a side view of the famous smile; he is dressed in blue jeans, cowboy hat and ochre-colored ski jacket. The camera zooms in for a close-up of his face, and this snapshot-like image of

Matt is moved to the upper left corner as the words appear graphically on the blue screen: "SOLID, EFFECTIVE, WORKING FOR MAGIC STATE."

A male announcer provides the voice-over for the spot. There is no music. He speaks clearly, neither quickly nor slowly, but keeping pace with the visual movement of the spot.

> We elected Matt Niceguy to the U.S. Senate because we knew he'd work hard for Magic State, and he did. Let's look at just part of what he's done. Niceguy protected Magic State's water from federal interference. He's leading the crucial fight in Washington against a federal lid on our local widget tax. He's leading the effort to ban exploitation of the Magic wilderness. Niceguy wrote the law protecting small businesses and ranches. Matt Niceguy. SOLID, EFFECTIVE, WORKING FOR MAGIC STATE.

The reassurance spot also tells a story. The audio portion features the voice of Matt Niceguy over a guitar softly strumming. Matt is describing the needs of the elderly in America. His voice is calm, confident, reflective: "The elderly of America do need reassurance on a couple of levels. One is that their contribution has been recognized. That we know that they did do something to make things better for us. And they need reassurance from the political structure of the country that their social security is not threatened. We owe them dignity. We are *not* going to walk out on those commitments."

Visually, the spot begins with a shot of Matt walking into a room where elderly people are sitting. One gray-haired lady stands to greet him, hugging him, smiling. She stands very close to him, her hands lightly touching him at the elbows. She introduces him to another elderly lady who rises to shake his hand. Matt is dressed in gray sport coat and gray slacks. The camera cuts to a shot of him seated in a chair. He is "at home" in a yellow and brown plaid shirt, talking straight into the camera, confidentially. The scene evokes a homey intimacy.

The camera cuts again to the scene of Matt with the elderly people, then moves to the face of the elderly woman smiling as she listens to Matt. Cut again to Matt talking, the camera's range of vision contracts to and then focuses on his hand reaching out to the elderly woman. Taking her hand in his, he gives it a reassuring squeeze.

The spots used in the first "flight" predominantly show Matt Niceguy at home in Magic State. (A "flight" is a series of ads aired together within a relatively brief period of time.) He is a man who disdains the trappings of power for the natural luxuries that the state has to offer. He is shown close to people, walking among them as well as leading them. And always there is the warm, open, smile. The look that tells viewers they are seeing straight through to the inner man.

In discussing the initial attraction stage of the courtship campaign, we introduced the notion of "reciprocity." The example of reciprocity cited earlier from Senator Niceguy's campaign showed how he understood the character of his constituency as well as they understood his character. In the building stage of his campaign, Senator Niceguy again relies on a display of reciprocity.

The spots aired in the second flight of advertising focus on a "performance reciprocity." These spots feature casework. They are best described as testimonials to Niceguy from ordinary people in the district. Typical of these is a spot that discusses the senator's efforts on behalf of a woman whose disability benefits were cut off. The spot begins with a medium shot of a middle-aged woman. She has reddish brown curly hair. She is solidly built, seated in a chair in her living room. The camera cuts to a full length shot of her walking down a grassy path. She is having obvious trouble with one leg, limping. Cut again to a shot of her at home, looking out the window, then turning and sitting, waiting.

The camera moves in for a close-up of the woman's face, the weariness, pain, disappointment, and longing of the years permanently etched there. Cut again to a shot of Matt and the woman walking down the same grassy path that the woman had walked alone before. Matt's arm is resting loosely about the woman's shoulders.

The symbolism of the repeated sequence where the senator walks beside the woman along the same path she had previously walked alone is subtle but brilliant.[25] It tugs at the heart before the viewers are even aware of how they may be interpreting the spot. The audio content of the ad is as unembellished as the visual. It is the simplicity, in fact, that gives the ad its punch. There is no background music. The voice of the woman begins: "I had complications and almost lost my right leg. The doctor's said I'd never work again." A strong male announcer's voice interjects: "Mary Hardwork is disabled but because she found a way to earn a small amount of money Social Security cut off her benefits. Senator Matthew Niceguy got them back." The voice of the woman completes the ad. Her voice changes from the undercurrent of desperation to elation. "I didn't know which way to turn. I went into Senator Niceguy's office and it was resolved in thirty days. Man I'm telling you I was on cloud nine. Senator Niceguy went to work and he darn sure fought for me I'll tell you."

The other casework spots hammer the same theme, although with different details. The audio is always the voice of the individual who has been helped, with only minimal use of the announcer. The visual images show the person helped, often with the senator. Always the senator is battling the bureaucracy on behalf of the ordinary citizen. The citizens seek help not because they are too feeble minded to solve their own problems. Indeed, they are all shown as rather fiercely independent, intelligent, but caught in the gargantuan bureaucratic web that entangles and obstructs the goals it was created to serve. Senator Niceguy is the knight with shining scissors who cuts through the red tape and clears the way for the independent Magic Stater to retain that independence with dignity. The qualities of his constituents which Matt Niceguy and his local staff spoke of so respectfully in discussing their strategy are interwoven in these testimonials. It would be impossible to create a deeper sense of identification or show more clearly the character of the people of Magic State.

Brad Show, producer for Matthew Niceguy, seems to have a penchant for latent symbolism. One of the spots produced for Niceguy features rainbows and is stunning in its symbolic appeal. The spot intricately weaves the audio and visual message. It begins with the voice of an elderly man: "I'm 80 years old. I've had to support myself since I was 11 years old." A deep male voice announces: "Everett Miner has some land claims he hopes to pass on to his children. Last year the Bureau of Land Management canceled his claims, the only thing he had of value seemed lost. Senator Matt Niceguy straightened it out." Miner's voice returns: "I went to Senator Niceguy. In four days the papers had been found. It is good to know that Senator Niceguy is working for people like me."

Visually, the spot begins with a medium shot of a weather-beaten old man dressed in clean white shirt and white cowboy hat. He is tying a horse to a tree. The camera moves back to show him standing beneath the tree, an old trailer in the background. The camera cuts to a shot of the old man walking along a mountainside. He stops to examine a rock, breaking it with a hammer he is carrying. This is a long shot that shows mountain ranges in the background and storm clouds gathering. As the announcer gets to the part where he is telling about Niceguy solving the bureaucratic snafu for the man, the camera shows the old man walking uphill, continuing to examine rocks. There is a long shot of a double rainbow arching over the mountains above the silhouette of the old man. The light is brighter as it appears the storm is clearing, not gathering. The last shot is of the old man standing in front of the tree in the same position as when the spot began. The tagline is the same as those in the earlier spots, "Niceguy. Solid, effective, working for Magic State." The upper right corner photo shows the senator shaking hands with Everett Miner.

The image of Senator Niceguy as a concerned and active representative is reinforced by this spot. Again, he is portrayed as involved in the individual lives of his constituents—a white knight battling the malevolent bureaucracy. His opponent is never mentioned. Senator Niceguy is running against the bureaucracy. His attacks are never answered by the Social Security Administration or Bureau of Land Management—nor will they be. His attacks are indirect—made through the testimony of the individuals he has helped. The presentation is subtle, symbolic, and highly effective because of its simplicity. There are no statistics to burden the viewer. Instead, the character of Senator Niceguy and his insights into the character of the state are revealed. The viewer is brought to intimacy with the senator through the endorsement of "friends and neighbors." The people featured in the spots could be anyone's neighbor, co-worker, relative, or friend. But they are never "generic." They embody the spirit of Magic State's people. We empathize because we get to know them and their problems.

A spot aired in the final days of the campaign takes a slightly different tack. Although it is indeed a testimonial, it features a United States senator from a neighboring state. The simplicity of the visual images of the spot underscore the sincerity of the audio message. The spot begins with a graphic presentation of the audio announcement of the senator. White letters appear on a lush green background. The camera dissolves to a head-on shot of the senator, short hair greying, framed against a chestnut brown background, seated in a high backed chair. The senator looks straight into the camera, serious but not solemn: a portrait of sincerity. The camera never wavers from this view throughout the sixty-second spot. The audio content of the spot is presented through the voice of the endorsing senator. A voice that is calm, confident, sincere, statesmanlike:

> I would like to speak to you, not just as a United States senator, but as a concerned citizen who believes there can be no more compelling goal than the reversal of the nuclear arms race. Your senator, Matthew Niceguy, is working for real reductions in nuclear arms. He's committed to peace and stability. But right now the Soviet Union has the edge in nuclear superiority and has refused to allow on-site verification by the United States. That's why Senator Niceguy and I oppose quick fixes that freeze nuclear arms. We must press forward with meaningful reductions. With nuclear weapons proliferating . . . worldwide, Senator Niceguy and I recognize the urgency of this issue. I serve with Matthew Niceguy. I know his record. Magic State is fortunate in having a senator of such dedication and ability. Thank you.

The endorsement spot, coming at the end of the campaign, indicates to viewers that not only is Niceguy close to them, one of them, but he is also accepted in Washington. He can be effective on their behalf because he is respected in Washington.

The sum of Niceguy's presentation of self is overwhelmingly positive images. By accident of birth he happens to possess many attributes regarded as physically attractive: he is tall, lean, with a warm and easy smile. The impression of his similarity to his constituents is reinforced in his dress and the settings of his advertising—all of which are identifiable with the state. His reciprocity of feeling for those who have previously elected him is testified to by ordinary people in the casework stories. As we have said, the incumbent need not devote time to sparking initial attraction, only to reevoking it. His concern is building on the relationship that already exists between him and his constituents.

Anatomy of a Challenge

The basic threats to a relationship between candidates and constituents include: 1) too many areas of dissimilarity (role expectation, values, behavior, interests), 2) boredom, 3) changes in reciprocal evaluations (the romantic spark is replaced by nagging criticism), 4) the presence of more desirable alternatives, and 5) perceptions of inequity in commitment, responsibility, or reward.[26]

Thus far we have focused on the positive aspects of building a relationship. As even the most casual political observer will note, however, campaigns are not always waged positively. Sometimes, regrettably perhaps, a suit is won by tripping the opposition. Candidates concern themselves not only with averting the deterioration of their own relationships with voters but with hastening the deterioration of their opponents' electoral relationships.

Deterioration of the political relationship begins when one or both parties view conditions as undesirable. Candidates may react in one of four ways when confronted with a deteriorating campaign—with "exit," "voice," "loyalty," or "neglect" behaviors.[27] "Exit behaviors" include actively ending the campaign, as when former U.S. Senator Gary Hart and Senator Joseph Biden dropped their 1988 presidential bids. The retirement of incumbents facing a difficult reelection also exemplifies exit behavior at its less sensational. "Voice behavior" involves working at improving the relationship. Stepped up constituency services, more visible media presence, and general attentiveness to the reelection coalition exemplify voice behaviors. Exit and voice behaviors are active.

"Loyalty behaviors" involve passively waiting for improvement. Loyalty behavior is best described as the reliance on past performance without present effort. Loyalty behavior begs the question, "What have you done for me lately?"[28] "Neglect behavior" is the candidate's passively waiting for further deterioration. In this instance the candidate (and his campaign staff) are seemingly immobilized, unable to act and awaiting the end. Neglect may be unconscious—as in the case of the senator too busy legislating to spend time campaigning. Both loyalty and neglect are passive behaviors.

The challengers' suits rest on their abilities to place themselves squarely between the incumbents and their devotees. One doesn't seek a new romance when satisfied at home. Thus, the challengers must present themselves to the public as a more desirable alternative. This is the first step in breaking the bond between incumbents and constituents. Most often, therefore, challengers adopt "contrast advertising" (negative or attack spots) as a necessary strategy. The reciprocity of the relationship between incumbent and constituents is already in place. This is not so for the challenger, and reciprocity is perhaps the easiest area in which an incumbent can raise doubts about his challenger.

In this the Niceguy-Goodchance race, the challenger perceived his greatest difficulty as establishing an independent, positive identity. Issue perceptions, which might have been used to help establish an identity, ended up being a negative force because his own issue positions were overridden by his identification with the national Democratic party and, particularly, by his prior association with Ted Kennedy. Revealing the quality of his character was a struggle never quite won for two reasons. First, a great deal of time and effort was expended simply to generate awareness of his candidacy statewide. Second, the incumbent was able to raise suffi-cient doubts about his challenger—i.e., by stereotyping him as a "young, ambitious, lawyer"—all three characteristics quite true but capable of carrying negative connotations. "Young" can connote a fresh outlook, or it can connote in-experience. "Ambitious" can connote progressive and for-ward thinking, or it can connote a lust for power. "Lawyer" can connote a familiarity with the law and the legislative sys-tem, or it can connote a shyster. The challenger could not deny that he was young, ambitious, or a lawyer. Connota-tions and subtle innuendo are difficult to answer.

In terms of strategy, the challenger and his producer agree that the two biggest obstacles they faced were the lack of money with which to wage a campaign and a lack of voter awareness of Goodchance's campaign. The two are not un-related. Better financing would have enabled Goodchance to get his message more efficiently to more people. And creating "name recognition" or awareness would have allowed him to spend time challenging the incumbent—as opposed to intro-ducing himself to the electorate.

Bob Goodchance and his producer B. McClure see the campaign in a radically different way from Matt Niceguy and his advisors. Goodchance and McClure see national forces at work, whereas Niceguy and his associates see the race as a local race. According to Goodchance, "the Republican slogan of 'stay the course' was what people wanted to do. There was a lot of concern about deficits, social security, but people weren't convinced that the Democrats would do anything about it. They thought Reagan needed more time and a Re-publican Senate to do it."

A major issue in the Magic State race was the negative tone that both candidates acknowledge was present in the race. Both candidates mention several spots as contributing to this tone, in particular a social security spot. Let us explore in detail the attack spots used in the challenger's campaign. For the moment, we shall leave aside the issue of the credibility of these charges.

Four spots designed to hasten the deterioration of the incumbent's relationship with voters were released by Robert Goodchance. They were a political quiz spot, a campaign contributions spot, a spot that attempted to challenge Matt Niceguy's identification with the state ("where's the horse?"), and a social security spot. Each of these spots relies on a male announcer to relay the message. Neither the voice nor the image of the challenger appears in the main body of the spot, however, a picture of Goodchance appears with the tagline at the end of the spot.

The political quiz spot is somewhat dull visually. It relies on white graphic letters on a black background to hold the viewers interest. A big red F appears superimposed on the screen at the end of the quiz. The spot ends with the still photo of Goodchance dressed in conventional suit and tie, wearing big thick glasses, unsmiling. The announcer says:

> This is a political quiz. Which one should a senator from Magic State support? Wrong. Senator Niceguy voted for tobacco price supports and against grain price supports. Now which of these should a Magic State senator support? Wrong again. Senator Niceguy voted for a tax break for himself, big business, and big oil, but against tax breaks to benefit middle-class people in Magic State. We think Matt Niceguy has failed this test. This time let's elect a senator who'll put Magic State first.

The contributions spot follows much the same format as the political quiz spot. The viewer is presented with a flattering photo of Matt Niceguy (in cowboy hat), smiling his famous warm smile. The photo is black and white. As the announcer speaks, a graphic list of campaign contributors scrolls up the screen in white letters. The spot ends with a big white question mark over Niceguy's face.

The audio content of the spot plays on anti-"Bigstate" sentiment common in many quarters across the country.

> Take a good hard look at this screen. What you're watching is a list of campaign contributions. You'd think this is a list of contributors to someone running in [Bigstate.] Someone very valuable to the big [widget] companies. Well, you're half right. It is a list of campaign contributions to someone very valuable to the big [widget] companies. But he's not from [Bigstate.] He's our own Matt Niceguy. Magic State's Niceguy. Or is he?

The third spot, "where's the horse?" relies on the same techniques visually as the ads described above. The screen is black except for a tiny box in the middle. The tiny box expands to fill the screen, revealing a black-and-white photograph of Matt Niceguy, smiling out at the viewer, wearing a white cowboy hat. When the photo grows to almost cover the screen the picture is turned over revealing another photo of Niceguy. This time he is dressed in a suit, still smiling. The photo turns over again, and now the original cowboy hat picture is side-by-side with the more formal picture. Both photographs are flattering to Niceguy. The audio content of the ad is considerably less flattering to the senator.

> Remember the guy on the horse? Yeah, that's him. The one who told you six years ago that he was going to charge off to Washington to fight for Magic State. Well, let's take a look at him now. Once Matt Niceguy got to Washington, he voted for big oil, big business, and himself. In fact, if you looked at his voting record you wouldn't know he's from Magic State. What happened to the charge? Where'd the horse go?

The social security spot provides more visual interest, but leaves unbridged the gap between the viewer and the elderly woman portrayed. The gap exists partly because we hear the words of an announcer, not the woman. This lends the air of "acting" to the spot—and inhibits the establishment of empathy. The social security spot also takes advantage of the use of color. Like the other spots, there is no background music to set the mood or enhance the message.

The spot begins with a long shot of a woman walking down a path from a farmhouse to the mailbox in the foreground. She is dressed in a simple brown cotton housedress. Her hair is severely tied back. She walks with a slow measured gait into a medium shot. She opens the mailbox and looks up at the camera (into a close-up) with disappointment. The camera studies the lines on her face, the workworn creases, as her hand reaches to her brow. She looks worried. She brushes a wisp of hair back with her hand. Her hand rests on the mailbox and she looks straight into the camera. Her mouth set in a distraught line. She turns to walk away. The camera follows her slow steps. At the bottom of the screen a graphic outline of mountains appear above the words, "Goodchance, U.S. Senate."

Accompanying the visual images of the woman checking the mail, a male announcer says:

> What if the checks stop? What if senators like Matt Niceguy finally won their battle against social security. All that stands in their way are tough individuals like Robert Goodchance, who understand and care. The fight will continue. Next year, and the next. But we can only be sure we'll win if we elect Robert Goodchance.

Aside from the family spot, the attack spots produced for the challenger would appear to be the most effective. Yet Goodchance was soundly defeated, and the credibility of his challenges to Senator Niceguy were widely questioned. Judging the impact of the attacks in the development of public perceptions of the challenger's style necessitates reconsidering the challenger's credibility. Why were some of the most powerful images of the campaign deemed unreliable sources of information by a preponderance of voters?

Although these could have been potentially effective attacks there are certain aspects of the execution that make them risky. First of all, some experimental research demonstrates that it is the visual message that dominates viewer cognition rather than the audio.[29] The use of flattering photographs of the incumbent senator may have led some viewers, who had tuned out the audio message, to simply have positive sentiments toward the incumbent reinforced. Even those with less positive attitudes toward the incumbent might be turned off by what appeared to be a highly personal attack against a man widely perceived to be warm, likable, and nice. Challenges in the other races discussed in chapters 4 and 5 demonstrate that the most effective attacks are those with subtlety. "Some senators," "the Washington crowd"—indirect yet meaningful ways of referring to the opponent that leave his name implicit are more effective than direct assaults. Finally, the contrast ads attempt to use a local image in a negative way even though that local image is highly revered throughout the state. The photo of the senator that dominates the "where's the horse?" spot is the one of him in a white cowboy hat. The imagery of the charge, and the horse, is one that is near and dear to the hearts of the people, and vital to the history and culture of the region. The pictures of the senator that are shown lead the viewer to conclude that he still belongs on his horse charging the bureaucracy. The visual images of the challenger presented in the spots used throughout the campaign do not show his connection to local values and culture.

Reflections on the Race

Two candidates for one seat in the U.S. Senate. Both are sensitive, compassionate men, intelligent, thoughtful, and reflective. Both are deeply involved in politics because of a sincere desire to be public servants, with the emphasis on service. There is much more to each man than the ads for either man revealed. The depth of their characters is illuminated in the way they put the race into perspective after it was over, reflecting on all that was done, and all that was left undone.

At the core of this campaign was the issue of attacks, negative advertising. Who said what, about whom, first? According to the senator and his staff, they made every attempt to take the high road.

> We absorbed them [attacks] for a long time. Didn't respond at all. And we found the press saying privately they admired that. But in tracking we found that they were working. So we came back using his own record [Goodchance's] and quotes. People came up to me and told me, "we were so glad you answered that. We were beginning to think it was true because we didn't hear from you." But overall we didn't respond to attacks.
>
> There were two attacks [on Goodchance]. One based on his association with Ted Kennedy and his liberal record. The other based on his voting record and attendance.
>
> One ad [response] featured [other Senator from Magic State] and sets the record straight about my votes on the congressional pay raise and social security.

For Matt Niceguy, reflection brings a bittersweet reminder of all he knows about the character of his people. The sense of decency which has been a staple of the local culture is fragile, too easily disturbed by the impact of outsiders—national party committees, outside media producers, and fierce political competition. When asked if there was anything he would change if he could run the race over again, he replied:

> Opponents. I want one like [other incumbent] got this year— a nobody. [*Laughs.*] Seriously, I was really upset by the behavior of the Democratic National Committee. They set the tone of the race. I knocked on seventy thousand doors and there has always been a sense of decency about things. You know, people were polite and listened to you even if they disagreed. On the last day I had one brochure left and waited for this old guy to help his wife into their pickup. I told him who I was and tried to hand him the brochure. He said, "I know who you are you son-of-a-bitch" and grabbed me by the throat and literally scratched the skin off until it was bleeding. That was really unsettling. That things could get so negative and so hateful.

In talking about his role in the race and his own attempt to take the "high road" Matt Niceguy argued that candidates can, and should, be responsible for the content of their ads. The price of victory may be too high. There are things he was unwilling to do:

> I viewed everything before it was aired. One ad was sent back to Brad Show because it was inaccurate. I wasn't going to let it get on the air when I knew it was inaccurate and would just have to be pulled. Tracking showed I was even, or down, and they wanted me to go on the air. But I said no. Joe and Brian argued with me and convinced me that we needed a response. A response *was* aired, but not the one the senator objected to.

The obstacles raised by lack of money and recognition are clear themes in Bob Goodchance's perceptions of the race. In terms of strategy, Goodchance's campaign needed to accomplish two things. First, he needed to reveal himself to the people of Magic State "as a man." Second, he needed to raise doubts about the incumbent "Matt Niceguy" and his connection to the state. His campaign was thwarted by a multitude of small production decisions made by his producer which hindered the translation of his message. His videostyle failed to communicate the essence of the man.

> [The campaign] became a credibility issue. Matt Niceguy said, "do you really believe I would vote to give myself a tax break in an election year?" We could probably have survived that problem if we had the money to do media in April.
>
> We probably got too negative the last two months of the campaign as a result of the things I mentioned—the social security issue and Niceguy's voting record. We probably could have more effectively used the issue of how he had changed, and supported that with the kind of stuff we had in the campaign cost commercial. We could have done a lot better job on the [widget] industry issue. We got too caught up in the social security and congressional tax break issues. But the issues were coming out so strong in the polls. We tied that into the so-called fairness issue. We talked about it in April, but then the last two weeks became, "who is telling the truth?"

For the challenger, Robert Goodchance, defeat is handled with grace and dignity. He too acknowledges that the price of winning, and serving, may be too great. The Bob Goodchance that is revealed in the family spot is the essence of the man. And the essence of the man is in his deep connection to his family.

> I would run it again if I had the kind of personal funding the race needed, and I'd do more in the media. All those mornings of getting up and traveling didn't mean anything. I'm convinced that people made up their minds watching TV commercials. Not even the press coverage. That's where minds are made up in large enough numbers to win elections. I'd start later, spend more money on TV earlier, and I

wouldn't have run the social security commericals, and I'd run the Magic State commercial more.

The campaign manager and I would joke at the beginning of the campaign about how Magic State was probably the only state in the union that you could still win a race by going out and meeting the voters and using the traditional old fashioned way of campaigning. After the race we both sort of laughed, because it wasn't true here anymore either.

In a way I'm sort of glad I didn't win. You know when we filmed the commercial of my son and I fishing. For weeks afterward he would say, "Dad, when are we going fishing again?" And I couldn't take him, obviously, because of the travel and the campaign. It was always, "after the campaign is over." . . . I think if I'd been elected it would have been the end of this marriage. I don't think the marriage would have survived Washington.

I'm not going back into politics. I quit shaving the day of the election, and just shaved my beard off last week. People say it means I'm getting ready to run for office again, but that's not true. My wife is very active. In fact, at the beginning of the campaign she said she'd do anything but public speeches. Well, the first time I had to be in two places at once, she went ahead and did it. Now she is very active, more than I, politically. She might run for something. I don't think I will.

Conclusions

What conclusions can we draw from the revelations of the campaign principals and from their ads? The race in Magic State pitted a popular incumbent of the majority party against a popular challenger running his first statewide race. Both candidates selected media producers from outside their state. Incumbent advantage, in this case, included a campaign staffed with a more experienced producer in addition to greater financial resources, greater recognition, and a public image that allowed him to co-opt popular values for the presentation of his message.

First and foremost, it is important to consider where the two candidates began their courtship of the electorate. The incumbent, Matt Niceguy, began with statewide recognition and approval. People perceived him as a warm, likeable, person—as one of their own. He was perceived not only as *someone they knew*, but just as importantly, *as someone who knew them*. The challenger, Robert Goodchance, began his courtship as an unknown. Unknown and, as such, untrusted. His attempts at establishing an identity, and trust (credibility), suffered both for financial reasons and because many of his spots failed to create for the viewer/voter a sense that they were coming to know him as a man. Matt Niceguy further enjoyed the advantage of fundamentally agreeing with the prevailing political philosophy in the state.

The images Matt Niceguy's campaign presented through televised advertising reinforced the positive base he had established in his 1976 campaign and also revealed his understanding of the character of his constituency. Robert Goodchance's campaign was unable to provide a comparable image of his understanding of the character of the state. The closest that he came to revealing his inner self is in the family spot. Had the Robert Goodchance who came across so clearly in that spot been connected to the state and its people through the rest of the campaign perhaps the hurdles to election would have been cleared.

The challenger's attempt to discredit his rival suitor fell flat, stumbling on the attempts at contrast. Matt Niceguy was able to distance himself from the attacks by having surrogates respond to the charges. The positive information his casework spots were presenting may also have countered any negative comments about the way he was performing in office. Furthermore, Niceguy was able to co-opt popular values in his campaign imagery early on, and thus focus the political agenda of the race on areas where he could win. While Goodchance spent his energy trying to defeat a popular incumbent of the majority party, Niceguy ran the race against the Washington bureaucracy. It was no contest.

Although the candidates began their campaigns at different stages of relationship development, physical attractiveness, similarity, and reciprocity were important to each. The audio, video, and production content of their spots was used to communicate each of these elements. Two themes are pervasive in the thinking of the campaign principals. First, both believe issue information was critical to their campaigns, though disseminated in different ways and at different stages of the relationship. Second, both feel the abilities of candidates and producers to create and sustain an emotional connection with voters is crucial to winning or maintaining political support. In the next two chapters, we will explore more fully the role of information and intimacy in the courtship campaign.

4

The Role of Information

Introduction

Chapter 3 followed the campaign process from the earliest stage of a relationship—initial attraction—through building and maintaining a relationship, to its continuation or deterioration and ending. We focused on tracing the development of the presentation of self through the various relationship stages and learned that candidates present themselves in different ways at different points in the campaign. Videostyles are influenced by the producers, since the candidates rely on them to put their messages on film or videotape. Two elements, information and intimacy, emerged as crucial in the thinking of the campaign principals interviewed in chapter 3. This chapter focuses on the first of these elements—the role that information plays in candidate videostyles.

Both of the candidates described here (we will call them Harold Doright and Johnny Fasttrack) began their 1982 campaigns with prior statewide campaign experience. Both candidates began the campaign in the "building" stage. The context of this race posed a threat to the incumbent because it fostered the perception of unequal commitment, responsibility or reward. The incumbent tried to counter that perception and to shore up his deteriorating relationship with a "voice" strategy. "Voice" was described in chapter 3 as the incumbent's strategy of reminding the voter/viewer of all that has been done for them, of a shared past. The challenger responds to the strategy with information that further encourages the voters/viewers to feel that they are less rewarded than the incumbent for having elected him six years ago.

The presentations of selves of both incumbent and challenger in this race relied heavily on issues. Issues were used to communicate similarity and reciprocity between candidate and consituency. While the candidates themselves dismissed the importance of physical attractiveness and of creating intimacy, their producers are less willing to do so. The ads themselves reflect the producers' philosophies in their production techniques and visual content, while echoing the candidates views in their audio content.[1] This chapter examines how issues interacted with the stages of the courtship relationship in the candidates' videostyles.

Political Setting

"Outland" is a sunbelt state with two to one Democratic voter registration. The governorship, both houses of the legislature, and most state offices have been traditionally dominated by the Democratic party. Over the past ten years, however, one can see some movement of Outland toward the Republican party in the increasing number of Republican candidates elected to the state legislature and to Congress. By 1976, the state's congressional delegation was evenly divided between Republicans and Democrats.

Although the state is becoming more competitive politi-

cally, Republican strength is unevenly distributed. The Democratic party remains strong in the northern and central part
of the state where most of the population is concentrated.
The southern part of the state, and one section of the largest
city in the state tend to favor the Republican party. The
state's natural beauty and idyllic climate have been responsible for the in-migration of large numbers of people from
other areas of the country over the past ten years.

In 1976 Harold Doright was elected to the United States
Senate by the largest majority a Republican candidate had
ever achieved. His campaign built on a national mood of
post-Watergate mistrust of government generally, and incumbents in particular. The theme of his 1976 campaign
had less to do with the ideological conservatism of the Republican party than the need to rebuild trust in government
through moral leadership. Integrity and change were the
central themes of his campaign, explicitly interwoven as
demonstrated in the audio portion of this spot aired in May
of 1976.

> On this day he will receive that rare gift-commitment. The
> opportunity to challenge, to change, to become Outland's
> representative in the United States Senate. He will talk of
> many things. Of a nation that must not look to the Mideast
> for its energy. Of a society that must not oblige the criminal
> for its safety. Of a clean environment. A productive economy.
> He will say we can face the world confidently with superior
> military strength, but that strength must come from that
> which is not simply military but moral. Real jobs must be
> created. Education standards made higher. This, not from a
> dreamer, but from a man of accomplishment. He is the be-
> ginning of what is good for Outland and America. We an-
> nounce with pride, Harold Doright for United States Senate.

The themes expressed in this spot were repeated in subsequent advertising throughout the 1976 campaign. The
subtle reference to Doright's previous public service record

refrained from a lengthy discussion of his past achievements (which might have been construed as arrogance) while still reminding people that Doright was someone who had already served his country, albeit not politically. Given public sentiments in 1976, this was perhaps the best possible background for a candidate running against an incumbent. Doright was squeaky clean, youngish but not immature, attractive, trim, and healthy looking. His opponent in 1976, "Senator Losttouch," had aged in office, gaining weight with the years, and seemed to have a penchant for issuing and then retracting statements throughout the campaign.[2] The incumbent senator's record had been tainted in the year preceding the race by investigations of his finances (which revealed no misconduct on his part) and negative publicity of his Senate performance. Doright's challenge to the incumbent Senator evoked negative perceptions of Losttouch without specifically naming him. Some examples of this tactic are to be found in the following ads.

Voice of announcer: He travels on roads that take him to the people. He has been to every county and will return again and again. He comes to listen. . . . He is challenging the old way. The limited horizon. The politics of corruption. The sadness of words spoken but deeds never performed. . . .

Voice of announcer: You're tired of a federal government that keeps overpromising. Not delivering. But somehow keeps raising your taxes higher and higher. You know we've got to start replacing those office holders who grow very fat and comfortable keeping things just the way they are. . . .

Voice of Harold Doright: . . . if we're going to have pride and confidence in our leadership, then suspi-

cions, doubts, and shady deals must go.
This change must begin in Outland, and
I think you would agree with that.

Voice of Harold Doright: . . . if we're going to stop crime in the
streets, we must stop all crime. Political
cheating, lying, beating the system. We
must have high moral standards if our
children are to believe in the system, and
if our government is to work.

Voice of Harold Doright:. . . . It's clear we have some very difficult
problems to solve. But in solving those
problems our basic values must remain
the same. Honesty, sincerity, really caring about people

The visual portions of the first ad feature Harold Doright
driving up to a group of people gathered out of doors, greeting them, shaking hands, placing a friendly hand on a
shoulder here, holding someone's baby there, tousling the
hair of a child. In the second ad quoted from above, the camera moves from a long shot of a woman in the parking lot
at a grocery store to a close-up of her face. She is Every-
woman—neither young nor old, rich nor poor, attractive nor
unattractive. She is darkly brunette, but not easily identified
as a member of any particular ethnic group. The third spot
features Harold Doright addressing a group of college students outside a campus building. The fourth spot—with the
text on crime—shows Doright addressing a small group of
middle-aged adults. The final spot shows Doright walking
through a barn with two old ranchers. Their clothes are
dusty, their faces lined. The important point about the visual content of the ads is that, in each case, it complements
the audio content and reinforces the theme that Doright is
trustworthy and will change government to make *it* more

trustworthy. By showing Doright physically close to and even touching people, the spots help to evoke perceptions that Doright is a compassionate leader, warm and approachable, yet strong.[3] Doright emerges in the ads as a great protector.

The audio, video, and production techniques of Doright's spots attempt to communicate the candidate's physical attractiveness, similarity, and reciprocity. Together they make up Doright's videostyle. Poll ratings of Doright showed that the dominant qualities Outlanders attributed to him during the 1976 campaign and subsequently were trustworthiness and honesty. By weaving these themes in the visual and audio content of the ads, Doright reinforced perceptions of his integrity and elevated its importance in the race.

Doright was seemingly riding the crest of a new political wave in the state, and to any observer this momentum appeared unstoppable. Preelection polling prior to his 1982 bid for reelection showed that Outlanders approved of his performance in office by about 70 percent. Yet the election returns indicated substantial declines in his political support over the course of the campaign. What factors accounted for the slippage in his popularity and political support? What was it about the 1982 campaign that rendered an ostensibly safe incumbent vulnerable?

The Incumbent's Perspective on Building a Relationship

In talking about the 1982 race, Doright refers to his 1976 victory. The six-year Senate term, in theory, insulates senators and allows them to be statesmen. (House members, on the other hand, face reelection every two years and must be constantly campaigning.) Despite Doright's large 1976 victory margin, he still sees himself as vulnerable.[4] The focus of his concern is how to use the time in office to solidify his political base, to build his new relationship, and to maintain hard-won political support. The initial attraction stage is not especially relevant to him since he is widely known and positively perceived. Perhaps because he is a Republican in a heavily Democratic state, perhaps because he entered the Senate by defeating a once popular incumbent, Doright sees the six years in office as having been a prelude to the next campaign.

> Our strategy started in 1976 after we were first elected. It was basically to serve the needs of the state of Outland in as visible a way as possible—first, through constituent service (we had the best constituent service set-up in the state) and, second, by working legislatively on those issues that are important to Outland as well as the nation. Then we wanted to project those accomplishments to the people. I spent a lot of time in the state personally. The last fourteen months before the election I was in the state every weekend but one, plus every recess. During the week I had to be in Washington. I was in Outland as much as possible and still be able to make the votes. We basically worked to make sure that the Republican vote got to the polls and then we appealed to conservative and moderate Democrats and Independents. I really don't have that conservative of a record.[5] . . . [We did] special projects, government projects like flood control, dams, land ownership. Of course, when a dam needs to be built you can't play politics with it. Projects were done because they had to be done. But we tried to let people know when we had been taking care of them.
>
> Once you're elected, you have to be responsive to the needs and aspirations of all your constituents. The question is: How do you balance the needs and aspirations of each group or person against the common good? What I have always looked at was how any individual or group request for assistance related to increasing individual freedom without interfering with the freedom of others, and related to a sound

economic policy, and related to the need for an adequate national defense. It turns out you can't satisfy all of the people all of the time . . . I was not the lackey for the bankers or the senior citizens or something like that. . . .

Senator Doright's 1982 campaign begins with building a relationship. There is no need for introductory devices to spark initial attraction such as those used in his 1976 campaign. Building a relationship is perceived and acted upon by Doright in two ways. First, the senator is concerned about the demographic composition of his support—who can he count on, and can he count on them enough to retain his seat? He knows that, as far as party affiliation is concerned, the numbers are against him. Thus, he must make explicit attempts to convert the unfaithful. This is accomplished through work on specific projects that meet the needs of the state and by "letting people know" when he has been taking care of them. There is an undercurrent of frustration in the senator's comment that, "you can't satisfy all of the people all of the time."

Deterioration

Senator Doright viewed his term of office as a time to prepare for the next election. While the above description of his constituency is largely in terms of demographic characteristics and issue concerns, the senator's insight into the personal character of his constituency is clear in this spot aired early in the 1982 race.

Voice of Harold Doright: The best way to describe Outlanders is that they are compassionate. They have all those characteristics that go with a people that like to touch, that like to talk, that like to help their neighbors. It is a

> spirit that has been born not only of the cultures that have mixed in our great state, but has been born of the frontier. People of the United States could not have survived without helping each other. And I think that spirit lives on and I believe it will live on forever.

This "frontier spirit" spot was aired from the beginning of the campaign until the end. From a positive focus on building upon his relationship, Doright's campaign slid rapidly into a deteriorating stage. As the senator began to respond to attacks on his voting record, the spot received less air time than it would have otherwise. In part, it was the political situation that lent a negative tone to the campaign, and helped Doright's challenger—Johnny Fasttrack—focus attention on the negative aspects of Doright's record. In interpreting the results of the 1982 election, Doright concludes that despite his strategy of concentrating his activities in office on issues, despite his campaign focus on issues, Fasttrack's effort to set up a negative information field on key issues was successful.

> In times of economic distress the Democrats are able to organize a larger base vote than they have in the past. The Republicans are either not prepared, or capable of, making that kind of organizational effort. The Democrats and their various special interests focused attention on Outland and [a neighboring state] effectively. We could see the results of that effort very effectively six weeks out. The early lead, which we knew would disappear, disappeared six weeks out instead of leveling out, which it usually does for Republicans. People who normally vote Republican don't turn out in off-year, nonpresidential-year elections. We spent two years trying to figure out how to counter that. Our phone banks were better organized, we put a lot of money into that. We used computers to organize the call lists, and we had good volunteers. We

just couldn't reach enough of the voters, who, if they voted, would have voted Republican. Because of the recession, the Democrats turned out. Organized labor was tremendously effective and, of course, their expenditures don't count because of federal election laws. Organized liberal women groups (liberal women are the only ones who are organized), environmental groups, the social security lobby, older people, believed the ads that the Democrats were using or just felt that over the long haul their financial interests would be better served by electing a Democrat. Particularly women's groups. They never had a senator who supported their interests as much as I did, but they organized against me. Environmentalists we didn't expect to get because we disagree on how to protect the environment—not on whether or not it should be protected, but on how to do it and create jobs.

Within the context of a poor economic climate, the challenger's negative information was more credible.[6] Later in the interview, Doright referred to the economy as being in a "depression" rather than in a "recession" (as above). This slip of the tongue may have been a more accurate description of the situation in Outland.

Senator Doright had not been in office long enough for constituent boredom to set in; in addition to which, he cut a somewhat dashing figure as a candidate. He had moderate-to-conservative views not unlike those of a majority of his constituents. His challenger was not, on the face of it, orders of magnitude more desirable as an alternative. Rather, Senator Doright's vulnerability stemmed from the troublesome state economy which may have given rise to the perception that there was an inequality in his relationship with constituents. Fairly or not, this perception might be bluntly articulated as "we gave him our trust and political support and in return got high unemployment." The perception of inequality of reward stimulated a deterioration in the political relationship in this case. The senator is aware that the economic context made him vulnerable. He also provides some insight into why a gender gap emerged in the support for his candidacy.

> Women are more concerned about income, men are more concerned about interest rates. There's about a 20–30 percent difference when you poll them. Whether you are a homemaker or a single woman, the most important thing is the paycheck. Men just tend to be less concerned until they lose their job. Women seem to feel more vulnerable.

Here again, the reason for slippage in support centered on issue information—not necessarily the issue one might expect women to base their decision on (equal rights), but on an issue of economic self-interest. Senator Doright sees issue information as contributing to his political vulnerability when coupled with a less than desirable political situation— an economic recession in the state.

Doright perceives his 1976 victory as a mandate to focus his Senate activities on particular issues. His discussion of the results of the race, his strategy, and his vulnerability are all issue-information oriented. In talking about how voters evaluate candidates, he also focuses on issue information.

> I don't think you can generalize [about how voters evaluate candidates]. It depends on education, how much they watch TV. *Most of it depends on how voters get their information.* I think voting record has relatively little impact unless it's used in a negative way. The Democrat's advertising showing me as against Social Security and the environmental issues was very effective. *It doesn't matter if its true, as soon as you have to start explaining you're through.* We tried to set up a positive base, but it didn't work. [Emphases added.]

Senator Doright sees the ability to process information (summarized by education) and the sources voters rely on for information as crucial factors influencing his political support. Issue information in particular was the centerpiece of his campaign. However, the record he established in office was less important than the need to explain it. Despite the fact that his 1976 ads provided virtually no issue information, he interpreted his 1976 victory as an issue mandate.[7] In that interpretation lay the seeds of deterioration. His personal image and approval ratings remained favorable throughout the campaign. The dominant characteristic he established as the key component of his image in 1976 (honesty) showed no diminution in 1982. Even when survey data showed vote switching, his approval rating remained strong. Let's take a look at the incumbent's 1982 videostyle and the tactics of his producer in hopes of explaining the senator's slide in political support.

The Incumbent's Producer

Out of fifteen ads produced for the Doright campaign only two attempt to re-evoke that base of trust so well established in 1976. The producer for the Doright campaign takes a strikingly different view of campaign strategy and voter evaluations of candidates from that of the incumbent.

Brad Show, producer for Matt Niceguy, also produced the ads for Hal Doright's 1982 campaign. The extent to which the spots reflect his personal political philosophy is very clear. Brad Show perceives the same strategic necessity for both Niceguy and Doright despite differences between them. The type of spots produced and the sequence of airing them is exactly the same for both candidates—even though Outland is two to one Democratic, while Magic State is heavily Republican. Doright is running against an opponent of the majority party with experience running a statewide race. Niceguy is running against a minority party opponent with no statewide campaign experience.

In talking about the Doright race, Brad focused more on

what was labeled earlier as the "intimacy factor" and seemed to view information as an important negative force in the campaign. According to this producer, the dynamics between Doright and his challenger, Fasttrack, created a negatively charged atmosphere that rendered the two spots attempting to reconnect Doright with his constituency ineffective.

Brad views the campaign process as an emotional connection rather than an educational mission.

> We wanted to reconnect him emotionally with the state.
> What we knew going into the race, from poll data, was that
> Hal Doright was thought of in a vacuum. If no one had op-
> posed him of any consequence he wouldn't have had to cam-
> paign. What he was missing was an emotional commitment.
> People thought he was a nice guy, but had no real reason
> to reelect him. He was regarded as somewhat aloof, some-
> one who had forgotten his home state and the people there.
> People didn't have any big problem, but they weren't in love
> with him. . . . Hal didn't do anything that emotionally. He's
> very goal oriented, just did his homework. That's important,
> especially in a state like Outland, where people tend to be
> fairly emotional. Our strategy was to come up with spots that
> put him in Outland, as opposed to Washington, with real
> people in Outland, saying and doing things with real people.[8]

The "emotional reconnection" is an effort to make the voters of Outland more comfortable with the incumbent. Issues are merely a device to cement that reconnection. The key to winning political support is controlling the agenda, setting up a positive field, then building on it. This strategy is built on a notion of different campaign stages or "tiers," each designed to evoke different feelings about the candidate. The first stage tries to set up general positive feelings toward Doright (reinforcing initial attraction), the second stage moves from the general to the specific, though still positive (building a relationship), the final stage introduces negative material (stimulating deterioration of the opponent's relationship).

There were three spots in the first tier, a sixty-second beauty. It talked about Hal and Outland as one and the same. It had pretty music and nice shots, some excerpts from interviews. It was one of the most effective spots. It was shown first in May, before the primary. The second spot was an issues laundry list—"accomplishments." It was supposed to remind people of his accomplishments on Outland-related issues. It was a thirty-second spot. The last spot in the first tier was "re-assurance." It was supposed to set up a positive field on the issue of social security. It was designed to inoculate people against social security attacks. We wanted to set up a positive field so people wouldn't believe attacks.

The first tier was designed to show Senator Doright as a physically attractive candidate who resembled his constituents in terms of political values. The use of key issues on which the senator and the Outland public agree was critical in showing similarity.

The second tier, using casework, was an attempt to communicate reciprocity, to depict the senator returning the affections of his constituents through service. The message was one of his intense involvement in solving problems confronted by the people of the state, and worked directly to address his vulnerability (the perception of unequal reward). Each tier of ads worked to communicate the senator's video-style in a single unified message.

The second tier took specific problems and had Hal solve them. We used actual casework examples. Picked issue subject areas that were of obvious importance to more than a few people—social security, retirement, disability, water in the southeast, the flood retention dam. It was an effort to carry reconnection with the state a step further, solving specific problems of specific people.

The third tier, negative advertising, is a decidedly risky strategy for an incumbent to undertake. However, it is quite common for candidates (both incumbents and challengers) to film an attack spot early in the campaign at the time of production and keep it "in the can." These negative ads may be used 1) in response to an opponent's attack, in an attempt to divert attention from his charges, 2) in a close race to put the candidate over the top, or 3) to stop a slide in support by showing the undesirability the opponent. In this case, the producer anticipated that negative spots would be needed, based on the behavior of the challenger during the Democratic primary campaign and on the political climate in the state.

> The first two stages were designed to make him lovable. We were hoping Jones [primary candidate] would win because he was widely regarded as an asshole. We were scared to death of Johnny Fasttrack—he was a more credible opponent. A far more tricky guy, more dangerous. He did things well in the primary that made us nervous. Tactically brilliant but uncalled for. [For example] he implied that Jones was hooked up with organized crime. Jones was too stupid to be much of a hood. Fasttrack took advantage of rumors, planted the idea that Jones was a crook, implicitly, subtly, brutally. Jones overreacted. Fasttrack was capable, and ready to do damn near anything to win the race.
>
> Doright was slowly coming down from midsummer on. Hard to tell what a heavy media campaign would do. Fasttrack was coming up. Fasttrack was doing a strident attack on Doright in personal appearances from late September on. Our inclination was to beef up his biography, keep our strategy. The pollster argued for attack. We didn't want to because it's dangerous for an incumbent. It's more accepted for a challenger to attack an incumbent.
>
> We thought about a quiz spot—which candidate will do this? By early October, the extent of the slide for Doright was such that it looked like he could lose. In a series of conference calls with Doright, his pollster, and his campaign manager, we were persuaded to do a negative attack. We stopped

the bleeding a little bit with radio spots which called into question Fasttrack's tactics. Fasttrack pulled his spots off the air, but didn't stop. He turned out a fresh batch of attack spots. The hardest was a social security attack. It became evident that we couldn't avoid attacks. Nobody questioned Fasttrack's attacks, no reporters asked why. He succeeded in setting up a negative atmosphere. Once that atmosphere is in place, positive media doesn't work.

The risk of negative advertising for an incumbent becomes clear in Brad Show's explanation of what happened when the negative ads were aired. There are basically three tactics an incumbent can use against his challenger. The first line of defense is to ignore the challenger, thus undercutting his credibility as a candidate. This tactic was used successfully by Senator Niceguy (chapter 3). The second line of defense is to encourage credible surrogates to attack the opponent—leaving the incumbent "clean" and distracting the challenger. Credible surrogates can include the press and other elected officials (the president, governor, congressmen in the state, the state's other senator, etc.). The last line of defense is direct attack from the incumbent. The reason this is a last resort is that the incumbent runs the risk of appearing "unsenatorial" and a bully. Negative advertising or contrast campaigning may be perceived as a legitimate tactic in only limited areas. Contrast advertising is hypothesized to be acceptable 1) when the area of contrast is relevant to performance in office 2) when the race is perceived as close and 3) when the contrasting information is perceived as true or accurate. If the incumbent (or challenger) steps beyond these bounds, he is likely to hurt only himself.

We did [a counterattack]. . . . Two things happened. First, it was so out of character with the Doright campaign. People were unaware that Doright was in a slide. Up to that point, Hal had been a good guy. The spots proved to be, in retrospect, not inaccurate, but sufficient gray area existed that questions of accuracy could be raised. Questions were raised by the press and by Fasttrack as to accuracy. We considered pulling them [the ads]. The campaign staff argued that they were accurate. What they were was legal. They [the ads] were perceived as bad sportsmanship. The perception was that the spots were wrong. Therefore, we figured that we had better do something or we're going to lose. The spots were beginning to take effect. Our solution was to pull the spots and replace them with a new attack, stronger, with less gray area.

Image Control: The Incumbent

Senator Doright and his producer, Brad Show, express different perspectives on the race. Doright is preoccupied with issues, with the record as a source of vulnerability when he is pressed to explain it. He sees the way voters choose to become informed, as well as their ability to process information, as crucial. Show is more concerned with voters' comfortableness with the candidate. He speaks in terms of reconnecting Doright with the state on an emotional level rather than educating the voters on the issues. In discussing the extent to which Doright's philosophy controlled the presentation of his image, Show contends:

> Doright, because of his nature and training, was more logically involved than he should be. Much more decisive, more apt to listen to his advisors when it made sense to listen. I admired his role in the campaign in that sense. When it came to decisions that only the candidate could control . . . [Doright] took an active role in deciding. Hal is bright, responsive, stayed very active in image control. His was a straightforward academic role. He was always involved though he did give [the pollster] and [consultant] control. We made suggestions and he would react to them. Adjustments were made based on his input.

Show's assessment of candidate involvement in the process of image development is similar to Doright's own assessment. Doright takes responsibility for the overall strategy and major decisions, including the important strategic shift that focused attention on negative information late in the campaign. According to Doright:

> I was responsible for the overall plan and major decisions, but I didn't run the day-to-day operation. In the 1976 campaign we had weekly staff meetings in which I participated, but that wasn't possible in 1982 because I wasn't [in Outland] during the week.
>
> I don't think there's any one person who exerted more influence than anyone else . . . the campaign manager, the pollster, and the media consultants, and I were the principals. Depending on what the decision was, I might bring in one or two others in a conference call, or occasionally in person.

Although Doright and Show agree about the degree of candidate involvement, the senator's description of the campaign philosophy is substantially different from his producer's view. For Doright, the centerpiece of the campaign, and his strategy, revolved around educating voters about his accomplishments in office. Subsequent to his election in 1976, Doright had begun to develop a plan for the 1982 campaign that revolved around constituency-service activities and Outland related special projects (what some might refer to as "pork barreling").

The Incumbent's Political Advertising

Despite Doright's intention of focusing the campaign on positive elements of his record, the activities of his challenger, Johnny Fasttrack, cast a negative light on key aspects of that record. Although both Doright and Show contend that it was the incumbent senator who controlled the development and presentation of his image, assessing the accuracy of that view demands a more careful examination of the ads themselves. Were they truly focused on issues? Did they contain the elements necessary for emotional re-connection with the state? Visually and verbally, what was the message that Doright sent his constituents in 1982 and how did it differ from his 1976 message?

The Incumbent's Political Advertising

For his producer, the strategic necessity of the campaign was *not* issue education but rather emotional connection. The ads Show described as being the "first tier" feature Doright talking about Outland (the "frontier spirit" spot was aired here), an announcer citing Doright's accomplishments in office, and Doright discussing the social security issue and his commitment to continuing the program. Each of the spots has the same background music, a piano slowly playing a single note at a time, very calming. Visually, each of the ads in this tier is similar. The shots are of Senator Doright with Outlanders in small groups. In many of the shots he is surrounded by people reaching to shake his hand or touch his shoulder. In the "reassurance spot" an elderly woman hugs him.

The spots in the second tier feature two Outland projects, one dealing with legislation which Doright had introduced and re-introduced until it eventually passed the Senate. It presents artist drawings of the Senate chamber as the bill was debated. There is no music in the background. The other special projects spot presents Senator Doright in his office sitting on a desk and talking about crime. As he discusses the impact of crime on the state, graphic bullets summarize his points on the screen beside him. This spot contains no background music either. Both of these spots are information dense—they contain a lot of factual information and statistics, as well as telling us the specific positions of Doright and mentioning his activities in solving the problems. Neither ad is particularly evocative emotionally. Both are only thirty-second spots, which makes retention of the information difficult. Although the spots contain many facts and statistics, the viewer is left with only a vague impression of what Senator Doright is accomplishing in Washington because there is so much information packed into thirty seconds. Neither spot addresses the most pressing issue in the state: extremely high unemployment and the economic recession.

Two other spots, which discuss "pork barrel" projects that Doright had brought to the state to help two communities, are much more evocative of the emotional connection between the senator and his state. Both involve water—a critical issue in Outland. The first spot deals with delivery of pure drinking water in a small community. The audio portion of the ad is spoken by a woman from the community. She and a member of a water commission speak of the severity of the water-pollution problem. The commissioner says that the people of the community were literally drinking sewage before the water project was complete. The woman says that Senator Doright is not a politician, but a neighbor and a friend. He acted out of concern for the people in her community, without asking for votes or political support. Senator Doright is featured in pictures, driving up in a pickup truck and talking with people, but his voice is never heard. It is as if we are catching a glimpse of him at work, looking over his shoulder without him knowing.

The second water issue spot involves flood control in another small community in the state. The mayor of the community had worked with Doright to get better flood control.

He died before the project was completed, and the spot features his widow talking about the project. Brad Show discusses the filming of this spot.

> When filming this ad, it was right after a rain storm in Flood-town. As they [the camera crew] got ready to shoot some film of the dam, there was a rainbow arching out from the commemorative plaque on the side of the dam, extending over the dam. This was significant because the mayor had died before the dam's completion. He had worked really hard with the Senator for it. He had been trying to get the dam built for years. The commercial is done by the mayor's widow. Great symbolism.

The "rainbow" ad is much more successful at emotional reconnection than the others. The widow speaks of how Senator Doright not only had the technical and political expertise to help the community but knew how much the project meant to the people of the community. The closing shot of the spot shows Senator Doright sitting next to her on the steps of her front porch as she reaches over and takes his hand.

The casework spots (three thirty-second ads) feature individual Outlanders talking about Senator Doright's assistance in fighting federal government red tape. One Hispanic man, a woman, and another middle-aged man are featured in the ads. Two of the spots deal with the senator's assistance to constituents in obtaining disability benefits to which they are entitled. The third spot deals with obtaining social security benefits. In the closing line of the ad, the man (seated next to his wife) says that if it weren't for Senator Doright, in all probability he wouldn't be around anymore. Each of these spots present strong images of Senator Doright as a compassionate and effective senator. They are simple in terms of production. The camera moves into people's homes, and they speak as if talking to a neighbor. There is no background music, no graphics, no special production features at all. The pace of the cuts between shots is moderate to slow. The camera lingers on their faces as they tell of frustrating battles to obtain benefits that are rightfully theirs. Voices crack as they reach the point of their stories where desperation sets in. Then hope and gratitude tinge the words as they tell of Senator Doright's intervention on their behalf. The senator's voice isn't heard at all. In only one of the ads is he pictured, visiting the woman whom he helped obtain disability benefits. It is the faces of these ordinary people that tell the story of an extraordinary man. Through his activities helping specific people with specific problems with which others can identify, the Senator is reconnected with the state.

The third tier consists of aggressive ads that contrast Doright and his challenger, Fasttrack. The "quiz" spot contains a rather flattering still photo of Doright and a rather unflattering photo of Fasttrack. While the senator's photo is displayed, the rich baritone of an announcer's voice presents Doright's voting record on balancing the budget and reducing taxes and spending. The words of the announcer are presented visually, captioning the picture. Then the photo of the challenger is shown, as the announcer declares that Johnny Fasttrack would raise taxes. The camera cuts to the photo of Doright and his record of bringing jobs to the state. Another cut to Fasttrack with a reminder that he is a "lawyer-politician" with no record on jobs. The final contrast is an endorsement of Doright by the other incumbent senator in the state juxtaposed to mention of Fasttrack's record of hiring consultants in other state offices he has held.

In addition to the "quiz" spot, two attack spots were aired which questioned Fasttrack's handling of a previously held office in the state. After this spot was pulled, another spot with essentially the same content, though much stronger in presentation, was aired. This new attack featured news clips and a statement by the governor reported in the press a year or more before that reflected negatively on Fasttrack's performance in office.

A Challenger's View

The two candidates involved in the race in Outland share similar views, while their producers are in agreement more with each other than with their clients. Fasttrack interprets the results of the race as an expression of policy desires, a mandate, if you will. In discussing his strategy, Fasttrack also focuses on issue information and describes the race as an educational mission.

> I think [the results of the 1982 election] can be interpreted as a statement that a [large number] of Outlanders were in agreement with me on the issues as opposed to agreeing with Doright. The issues we focused on were the economy and pre–supply side economic progress, social security, education, the environment, and level of defense spending. . . .
>
> We started out wanting to pick out key issues for the people of the state that a U.S. senator would have a role in. Then we wanted to draw a contrast with his [Doright's] voting record and the record I *would* have on these issues. . . . We only had attacks in the media, started getting them in the last couple of weeks. We felt they were factually inaccurate so we did one spot that responded. Through interviews I made the same point. I asked [Doright] on a TV debate to stop airing the ad, a week before the election. [The ad was changed.] Our response to the ad change was the same as the original. The ad was misleading, inaccurate, should be taken off the air. Our strategy was to draw the contrast on key issues. That's what our ads tried to do. . . . [Emphasis added.]
>
> Different ads were directed at different groups. The social security ad was important to senior citizens, people. I think we did fine. We had an ad on education funding aimed at

people with children and involved in education. We had an ad aimed at people concerned about the environment. The unemployment ad was aimed at people worried about losing jobs or people in the business community worried about the recession.

Fasttrack perceives the political support he received as a mandate for a change in political philosophy and direction of the government. He sees voters as concerned with issues and struggling to gather sufficient issue information to make a political choice, and he acknowledges the "intimacy factor" but dismisses its importance as "trying to convince the voters that you are a nicer guy." Fasttrack and Doright share the same overriding concern with issues and the same sense of a compelling mission to inform the public of their stands.

> I think they [the voters] are trying to cut through all the verbiage to find out who shares their priorities and values as to what the solutions should be. There are sort of two theories on how to run a campaign—one is to try to be a nicer guy than the other guy. The other is to talk about the issues. The overriding message we tried to get to the voters was my position on the issues. I didn't spend time trying to convince them I was a nice guy.

Orchestrating a Challenge

Richard Barber, Fasttrack's producer, is an experienced political campaigner. He organized a youth campaign for a presidential candidate in California in the 1960s, worked with various community development programs and a number of local campaigns (such as legislative and school board races). He has served as an advisor and campaign consultant to Johnny Fasttrack since 1970.

According to Fasttrack's producer, there are difficulties inherent in an approach that dismisses "trying to be a nicer guy." He talks about Fasttrack's style and his image.

> His style is so cool that people forget who he is. When he finished being [another state office] only 48 percent knew who he was. Of those 48 percent, they all thought highly of him. . . . One of Johnny's assets was that Johnny came from a middle-class family that has a gift for making money, which he didn't have any particular use for. And he was willing to spend it on a Senate race. . . . In the conduct of [previous office], the main thing expressed was his evenhandedness. To be as fair as humanly possible. He doesn't get mixed up in the partisan stuff. He's never criticized anyone in public and almost never in private. His image is, whatever all the other politicians are doing, do something else or don't do it. There's a story that illustrates that. The gridiron dinner that the press throws during the (last) race. We were sitting at a table and a woman that was organizing it came up and said he was to go up with the other candidates. They wanted him to do a can-can and sing a little song: "2-4-6-8, we are all the candidates." Johnny turned to me and said, "I'm not going to do that." I said, "I don't blame you, I wouldn't either," so we left. He doesn't follow the crowd.[9]

Lest one start to believe that Fasttrack is always a model of decorum and a lone representative of dignity among otherwise undignified politicians, it should be mentioned that during the senatorial race, both candidates, as well as several others running for office in the state, participated in a cowchip throwing contest. This event better symbolizes the rowdy, colorful, rough-and-tumble politics of Outland than the walkout on the can-can and song routine.

In contrast to Fasttrack's view of the campaign, centered on informing voters of issue positions, Barber, his producer, sees the issues as relatively unimportant—with the exception of the economy. It is the candidate's personal qualities that are his chief marketable "commodity."

One of the premises that I operate from is that people don't admire politicians. Period. Johnny is well admired. It was a key factor. I think of that as a commodity we protect and express. Johnny calls some things cheap shots. We don't do that. That's built in. You know sometimes when other politicians run around making a big deal of one thing or another. Johnny won't do it.

Someone told me once that issues have a life cycle of ninety days. I bet that's true. After the economy. You can find out how voters feel at a particular time, but they will reply to you in political terms. You look at what you think the poll results mean, decide what positions you can live with, and look at your opponent's positions and figure out where he went wrong.

Here we have another interesting contrast in views between candidate and producer. The candidate sees the issue positions as an expression of his own political values and philosophy. The producer sees the issue positions as the candidate's restatement of public opinion, derived through opinion polling. What the public expresses in admiration for Fasttrack results in a self-portrayal of those qualities that voters admire. Barber sees establishing Fasttrack's "cue-value" as important. Distinguishing him from his opponent chiefly involves "figuring out where he [Doright] went wrong." As already noted, in the six years of a Senate term, any incumbent will cast some votes which strike a discordant note with a heterogeneous constituency. If the challenger can effectively focus attention on these issues, he can control the agenda. In controlling the agenda, the challenger is able to express his own strengths and expose the incumbent's weaknesses. The philosophy Barber describes permeated the strategy used in the production and airing of Fasttrack's spots.

Outland is two to one Democratic, but they continually elect Republicans. There are two steps you have to take. Establish what they [the voters] are interested in. We did some in-depth polling . . . [Smith] was the key person. He's a really hot Eastern type. He was tough. Johnny and I are both kind of mellow. But he was tough. He urged us to be really tough, just go all out.

. . . We had negative education spots of Doright's record on five issues (social security, environment, jobs, education were the big ones). We ran two tracks—Johnny positive and then we'd trail it with the negative. We started positive over a ten-day run in September. . . . We had a monitoring system to track when spots were aired. Radio and TV spots were matched. One day Mrs. Fasttrack was home sick with the flu and was watching TV and noticed that we had bought time on a show and the spot wasn't aired. She called me up and said, "Hey, weren't we supposed to have a spot on?" So we set up the monitoring system. Without that, you buy the time and really have no way of knowing if the station is actually airing the spots. We sent out programs for how they [the spots] were to be played. Then we sent out the money.

We thought someone at one of the stations was for Do-right because we started getting response spots on issues we hadn't even run yet. They started their onslaught before we even ran ours. They overreacted. We knew we caught the old boy's attention. In [Doright's response] Fasttrack's name was mentioned seven times. I counted them as I listened to a radio spot on my way to the office. I realized then that they weren't on top of their game. They were twenty points ahead at the time. From that point on, it got worse. Show did Do-right's ads. They are known for their negative stuff. There's a different dynamic in a state this small. There is an ethic that says you can take someone on the issues but not personally.

. . . Then there was an image spot, sixty seconds, where Johnny summarized the issues and a thirty second biog-raphy where he talked about his past experiences and work in [previous office]. Then there was a spot with Johnny and Barbie [Fasttrack's wife] swinging their son with the song "A dime ain't worth a nickel anymore." In theory we would play the soft stuff first, then as the campaign got under way, bring in the negative first and trail it with the positive in both TV and radio. We wanted to concentrate on a single issue at a time. Three spots, social security, education, and jobs, got the most play on TV. . . . Part of our response to [Doright's attack] was a testimonial by [other public figure]; it played two markets heavily. We had a Johnny positive response, where he went on the air. We finished up with the big three—mostly education and social security. We continued to play jobs, but not as much. Social security was played the most, then it was a tie between education and jobs. The sixty-second image spot played daytime at the end.

Fasttrack and Barber are not completely at odds in terms of how they think voters evaluate candidates. There is a twenty-point difference between the polls conducted for the challenger and those conducted for the incumbent—which unfortunately remains unexplained. Again, while Fasttrack tends to dismiss the intimacy factor, Barber acknowledges the duality of influences on constituency building. While Fasttrack describes the process of evaluation as voters "cutting through the verbiage" in search of political values and issue priorities, Barber sees intimacy as a first threshold which the candidate must cross—afterwards working to establish issue closeness with the "visceral vote."

Politics are really embedded in America, including nonvoters, who make a big point out of nonvoting even on the negative side. Everyone has a point of view that's political. Voters are pretty shrewd. There's the point at which they choose between the candidates, and whether or not to vote. Then they decide what issues to vote on. If you're right on six out of ten things, they'll vote for you.

There is, broadly speaking, the personality issues. In some cases it might be trivial—is he good-looking? But mostly it's things like honesty, trustworthiness. In most cases the chance for voters to get to know the candidate is pretty rare. Mostly they do it through campaign communication.

If you look at any given campaign in almost any situation, you have those who aren't registered, so you don't have to deal with them at all. They are women, minorities, and the unemployed. It's sad, but true. You have 40 percent who are for you because you're a Democrat, or they're for the incumbent because he's the incumbent. The campaign battle is over 20 percent that you're trying to divide. George Will said the battle for politics is always for the shifting middle. What I call the "visceral vote." There's a lot of move to that vote. They tend to be the most influenced by a campaign to begin with, particularly media campaigns.

. . . The variable in elections, and what you never know, is who's going to vote. Since turnout is a key factor in a close race then you must reduce the risk. You have to make sure that those you can rely on to vote, vote for you. We tossed all the precincts in a computer and let the computer tell us which ones would vote Democratic. We had five contacts per household to get turnout. That's not the most that's ever been done. [Another candidate] did fourteen contacts per household when he ran for governor last time.

Barber sees issues as important, but contends that the life cycle of any given issue is relatively short—ninety days—except on economic issues. Therefore, since campaigns last longer than ninety days, building a campaign around an issue is difficult. Still, it is not impossible if the issue is carefully chosen. Once the "personality issue" lays the groundwork for the candidate's credibility, all that remains is the struggle over the moveable vote. A certain percentage of the potential constituency is disregarded outright because they are not registered.[10] Another group is conceded to the opposition without hesitation.[11] The battle is over a small group who are influenced by the campaign messages.[12] What matters for them, once a threshold of awareness has been established, is that the candidate be right on "six out of ten" things. As noted earlier, being right on the issues can be controlled by the candidate, once the polls tell him what the public wants to hear, and once the incumbent's record is scrutinized for vulnerabilities.

Image Control: The Challenger

Again, both candidate and producer agree on the extent to which Fasttrack controlled the presentation of his image. When describing his role in the campaign, Fasttrack stresses his involvement in actual production decisions, as well as decisions on scheduling and frequency of airing.

> I approved the running of every ad we ran. I had a lot to do with the scripting and production. We didn't allow anything to be shown until I had agreed to it. A lot of detail was handled by people on the campaign staff . . . Barber [was a big influence] on media advice, and Bobby on media. My wife was very involved in the whole process.

In discussing the control Fasttrack exerted over the campaign, his production consultant, Barber, also attributes final decisions to Fasttrack. Barber discusses how the ads were written.

> We wrote the scripts in the airport. Just finished seeing [a media consultant]. Johnny was on a roll, [he] just started going on this stuff. He wrote the positives and [pollster] and I wrote the negatives. Johnny viewed all the ads before they were aired. . . . As mild mannered and humble as he might appear, he makes his own decisions. He and I agree most of the time. The only disagreement we've had is over nuclear power.

Fasttrack and Barber both see the campaign as having been essentially positive. Negative information was provided, but always trailing positive spots. The candidate himself is seen by both as the one who controlled his image. The candidate, however, puts much more emphasis on issues than does the producer. Fasttrack dismisses the importance of the intimacy factor, while Barber minimizes the portion of the electorate that is capable of being moved on issues. By looking at the actual content of the ads, we can determine whether the producer's view, or the candidate's view, of the campaign process prevailed.

The Challenger's Messages

Twelve ads were released by Fasttrack for this study. The ad described by Barber as an endorsement of Fasttrack by another public figure was not included. The "biography" spot resembles the spot run by Doright in 1976 when he first ran for office in Outland. It features pictures of Johnny Fasttrack in what appears to be a campaign office, talking to people. Fasttrack is shown with shirt sleeves rolled up, moving around the room, talking with a variety of people, shaking hands as he approaches them. They are half smiling, half serious. The people he is shown with include men and women, young and old. An announcer's voice declares:

> When a man is running for the United States Senate, it's important to know something about him. Johnny Fasttrack grew up in a small Outland town. He won honors as an Eagle Scout, was elected student body president in high school, was graduated with honors from college, and went on to law school. He practiced law in Mountainview for ten years where he now lives with his wife and son. Johnny Fasttrack is currently [state office]. He'll make a fine U.S. Senator.

The second "image" spot Fasttrack aired touches on a number of issues, as a similar spot in Doright's 1976 campaign had done, but not in a way that states Fasttrack's solutions to those problems. It features Fasttrack talking, voiced over pictures of him walking and talking with people—again, young and old, male and female, working or middle class.

> Every day in this campaign for the U.S. Senate, as I talk
> to people around the state, the need for strong leadership
> is clearer. I want to be Outland's senator because I believe
> people do have a right to expect something from government.
> Social security is a great achievement. It will be tough, but
> it's a promise we can keep. We need to keep working for a
> clean environment. Because clean air and clean water are
> not luxuries, they are necessities. Even in our worst eco-
> nomic difficulties, we cannot allow millions to go without
> work. The fact is, the economy can't work when that many
> people are not working. Education is vital. This generation
> deserves the best education we can give them. We need a
> strong defense, but Lord knows it's no weakness to want an
> end to the threat of nuclear war. These are things that are
> important to me and to Outland. . . .

Another "image" spot, which deals less with personal characteristics of Johnny Fasttrack than with his performance in a previously held office, is also in the series. This spot begins with a close-up of Fasttrack, and then the camera slowly moves back to reveal a group of people sitting around a table in an office, talking. Between shots of the group, the camera moves in for close-ups of Fasttrack frequently. The announcer talks about Fasttrack's handling of five different issues while in office. The spot lasts thirty seconds.

The issue spots that received the most air play in the Fasttrack campaign and that are most typical of spots used in other races in 1982 include ones on social security, jobs, and education. Fasttrack's producer, Barber, claimed that there are positive and negative spots for each issue. The spot designed to present Doright's record in a negative light is clearly identifiable.

Have you seen Senator Doright's commercial crediting him with protecting our social security benefits? Fourteen thousand older Outlanders depend on minimum social security benefits to help them make it through each month. Senator Doright voted to eliminate those benefits three times, and he didn't change his mind until President Reagan backtracked. Johnny Fasttrack would always vote to preserve social security benefits intact.

The other social security spot may be more subtle, but it still has a distinctly negative tone. It features Johnny Fasttrack facing the camera head-on, dressed in a suit. The camera never wavers from the close-up throughout the thirty-second spot.

I'm Johnny Fasttrack. For forty years our older people have had confidence that the benefits promised them through our social security system would be there when they needed them. These benefits provide help to 36 million elderly Americans. Yet *some people* in the United States Senate have voted to cut these benefits. I don't agree with that. If I'm elected, I'll vote to maintain our social security retirement benefits intact. [Emphasis added.]

The education and jobs spots have similar tones.

Announcer's voice: Senator Harold Doright has put out a lot of commercials telling how much he has done for education. Well, if he's done so much for education, how come he voted to cut federal funds for student financial aid? How come he voted to cut guaranteed student loans? How come he voted to cut higher education benefits for children of veterans who died of service connected disabilities? Johnny Fasttrack would have voted the other way. The question is, how would you have voted?"

Candidate's voice: I'm Johnny Fasttrack. Today in Outland we have 60,000 people out of work. More people looking for work than live in Sun City or Cloudview. Miners, construction workers, office personnel, many other skills going to waste. Yet some in the U.S. Senate put a lot of other problems ahead of putting people back to work. I don't agree. If I am elected, my top priority will be jobs for the people of this state.

These spots were aired primarily during the daytime in the last few weeks of the campaign. Visually, the education ad features Johnny Fasttrack with his wife and son. The spot consists of medium shots of Barbie and Johnny Fasttrack swinging their son, with Johnny's words voiced over the film. The visual elements of the spot are unrelated to the audio. In the audio portion of the ad, each of the themes Fasttrack sought to use in his campaign are woven together. It isn't clear how Fasttrack will, if elected, ensure a quality education for every child, guarantee a full economy, or protect the solvency of the social security system. But the political values of the local citizens are expressed, and Fasttrack shows his agreement with those basic values.

The final spot that merits discussion is the response spot which features Johnny Fasttrack seated, head-on, addressing the charges the Doright campaign made against him in its two attack spots. Visually, the response ad shows a close-up of Fasttrack gazing sincerely into the camera, replying to each of the charges made by the Doright campaign, with the tagline "I regret Senator Doright's exploitation of these issues for his own political ends." The response was effective in that it was a direct answer to direct charges leveled by Doright at Fasttrack. The reply was made through the same medium as the charge. Since the charge came directly from Doright, it was appropriately answered only by Fasttrack.

The reply came quickly on the heels of the charge, diminishing the effect of the attack.

Other ads in the sequence released by the Fasttrack campaign dealt with local issues. They are interesting because of the taglines used. One ad concludes a discussion of another of Senator Doright's votes while in the U.S. Senate with the announcer asking, "So, we have a meaningful choice on election day, don't you think so?" (This ad was all graphic displays of the message as spoken by the announcer.) The other spot concludes a discussion of the positions of the two candidates, as reported by Fasttrack's announcer, by saying, "It's an honest difference between two good men. Vote for whichever one you agree with." (Visually this ad featured scenery of Outland.)

Verbally and visually the Fasttrack ads present different messages. The verbal messages are either hard-hitting attacks on Doright's record or attempts to associate Fasttrack with the traditional positive values of Outland's citizens. Visually the spots present Fasttrack as a devoted family man and an energetic worker, as a successful and well-liked person. Most often the setting for the ads is an office—linking Fasttrack to his work. Most of the ads feature Fasttrack talking directly to an audience. None of the ads released uses music, despite the mention of a particular tune by the producer of the ads. The production of the ads is as simple and direct as the audio message. There is limited use of graphics or other special production techniques.

Fasttrack and his producer disagree to some extent on the relative importance of information and voter intimacy with the candidate during the campaign. The candidate dismisses "trying to be a nicer guy," while the producer sees the importance of "personality issues," and recognizes this dimension as a hurdle to be crossed. Both Fasttrack and his producer attribute the negative tone of the campaign to the incumbent, however, it is clear from the sequence of the spots aired by each candidate, and the content of those ads, that the challenger was first to go on the offensive—at least through advertising. (Disentangling what was said in personal appearances, and when, is an impossible task at this point.) It is the challenger's philosophy which dominates the audio content of the ads. The visual elements of the ads reflect the influence of the producer.

Conclusions

The Outland race fits the general notion of the campaign as a courtship. The two candidates, Hal Doright and Johnny Fasttrack, skip lightly over the initial attraction phase since both have experience running statewide. Their energies are focused instead on building a relationship. Establishing similarity with the constituency, especially on issues, is seen by both candidates as a critical element of their videostyles. The producers for both candidates acknowledge the importance of issue similarity, but extend their concern to attractiveness and reciprocity as well. The influence of the producers' philosophies is most apparent in the visual content of the ads.

There are interesting commonalities in the views of incumbent and challenger, and disagreements between candidates and their own producers. Most striking is the concern of both candidates with issue information. For the challenger, it is issue information that gives credibility to his candidacy. The educational mission of his campaign lies in presenting his potential voting record in contrast to the incumbent's actual voting record in a convincing way. The content of the challenger's ads reveals that this translates into the liberal use of issue valence associations combined with attacks on the incumbent's voting record on key votes with which he believes the voting public will disagree. In presenting his own message, the challenger successfully co-opts widely held values, values that imply a promise for the future.

The challenger's philosophical emphasis on "pure" issue information and disdain for "trying to be a nicer guy" is tempered by his producer's philosophy that, with the exception of the economy, issues have a life cycle of ninety days. Obviously, as the campaign lasts considerably longer than ninety days, issues must somehow be interwoven and their lifecycle extended. In the challenger's case, what weaves together the issues are *values*. Public opinion is the acknowledged guide for the challenger on issues and values. What is critical is not becoming a mirror image of the public but being right on "six out of ten" issues. The challenger's producer is also willing to use a broader definition of "issues" than his candidate. The producer speaks of "the personality issues" rather than "trying to be a nicer guy." The candidate's own stated disdain for "trying to be a nicer guy" is not reflected in the actual content of the ads, which attempt to make an intimate connection between him and his potential constituency, and, in short, to portray him as a "nicer guy."

The unique feature of Johnny Fasttrack's strategy is not the content of the political spots that were produced but the sequence in which they were aired. Indeed, some of the tactics employed by Fasttrack in 1982 against the incumbent Senator Harold Doright had been used by Doright in 1976 in his challenge to Senator Losttouch. By implicitly linking the incumbent with "some in the U.S. Senate" and highlighting certain of his own values ("it's no weakness to want an end to the threat of nuclear war"), Fasttrack is able to use information in a challenge that defies reply. It is information that makes the challenger credible. It is information that makes the incumbent vulnerable. The ordering of spots, with positive information about Fasttrack trailed by negative information about the incumbent, helps to avoid tainting the challenger as overly negative. The campaign becomes a brawl which he appears to be above.

Although the incumbent sees information as the key to his strategy, it is in a different sense than that discussed by the challenger. For the incumbent, the campaign is an educational mission—"trying to let people know when we had been taking care of them." The record becomes a source of vulnerability because he is called to explain it, and explanation appears to fall on inattentive or unpersuaded ears. The incumbent believes that it is the way people seek information, and their capacity to process it, that influences their decision-making. In the six years spanning his campaign as a challenger and his first attempt at reelection, much about his style is changed. The information provided in his ads becomes more concrete. He moves from the discussion of values to the discussion of casework. Part of this change is the result of the perspective that serving in office lends to the campaign. Allowing the challenger to usurp the discussion of values however, causes the incumbent to relinquish some control of the campaign agenda.

The incumbent's producer has a perspective on the campaign that again alters the emphasis given to specific issues in the actual content of the ads. For Brad Show, the campaign is less an educational mission than a chance for emotional reconnection. He boldly claims:

> Voters don't evaluate candidates. In Outland, they wanted a guy, first, who had their interests in mind rather than national or international issues. Second, they wanted him to reflect local pride in the state. They want their senator to reflect that uniqueness in the state.

The sequence in which the incumbent's ads are aired reflects the stages of the campaign. First, the ads attempt the emotional reconnection of Doright with his constituents.

They then move to solidify perceptions of the incumbent by increasing the information available and making it more concrete—showing the senator helping specific people with specific problems (reciprocity). The third stage reveals that control of the political agenda has slipped from the incumbent to the challenger as negative information begins to be introduced. Charges are replaced with countercharges. The senator's previously established base of positive perceptions is neglected as the incumbent struggles against a slide in voter support. And though his approval level remains high, vote intentions begin to change. Though personal ratings remain high, support declines. The incumbent begins to discover that personal trust does not necessarily translate into political trust unless integrity is the focus of the political agenda. To win, he must shift the focus of the campaign back to qualities that constituents found so appealing in 1976.

The information voters receive throughout the campaign and the way they process it are indeed critical.[13] Although the candidates' issue concerns are not misplaced, neither is the producers' willingness to tinker with "pure issue information" in producing the ads. "Something more" than issue information affects the voters' ultimate evaluation of candidates. That "something more" is what another candidate labels the "comfort factor."

5

The Role of Intimacy

As important as issue information is, it alone cannot convey all that the voter/viewer wants to know prior to choosing a candidate. The crucial element that lies beyond issue information is intimacy. This chapter looks at a contest that pitted an admittedly attractive and warm challenger against an incumbent widely perceived as vulnerable because of his own lack of personal charm. The threat to the incumbent's relationship with his constituents can be described as being due to "the presence of a more desirable alternative." The incumbent acknowledged the potential threat early in his bid for reelection and actively worked to counter that perception. The challenger effectively helped set the agenda—personal character dominated both campaigns' messages. However, when the incumbent aggressively responded with strong and persuasive messages about his relationship with his constituents, their shared past and the prospects for the future—the challenger was left "speechless."

In the case examined, the videostyles of both incumbent and challenger relied on building intimacy. Similarity was conveyed through personal information, and reciprocity was communicated through shared values. Producers for both candidates were local, and thus, extremely sensitive to local tastes. This chapter examines the creation of intimacy in the relationship between candidates and voters through candidates' videostyles.

Political Setting

In 1976 voters turned nine incumbent senators out of office, more than in any other election year since 1958.[1] Although incumbents suffered at the polls, the balance of power between the Democrats and Republicans remained virtually unchanged. Ten of the freshman senators were Democrats; eight were Republicans. (Prior to the 1976 election eight incumbents retired—the highest number since 1960. Four of the retirees were Democrats, four were Republicans.)

Senator Daniel Cloistered from Sunstate was first elected in 1976, among the eighteen newcomers to the Senate. While not favored to win that race, he proved himself to be a formidable campaigner, defeating the primary favorite by a margin of two to one. Daniel Cloistered shared the squeaky-clean image of Harold Doright. In 1976 he waged an aggressive campaign against the incumbent, attacking him as a big-spending liberal who did not represent the attitudes of Sunstaters.

Prior to the 1976 campaign, a number of scandals rocked Washington and the nation. Perhaps these were the result of a heightened sensitivity to corruption brought on by the Watergate revelations, or perhaps they resulted from the close scrutiny of incumbents inevitable in any election year.

Indicative of the pervasiveness of scandal: Congressman Allan Howe (D., Utah) was arrested for soliciting. Representative Horton (R., NY) was charged with speeding and driving while intoxicated. Congressman Sikes (D., FL) was reprimanded by the House Ethics Committee for stock disclosure conflict of interest. Congressman Helstoski (D., NJ) was indicted for soliciting and accepting bribes to keep Chilean and Argentinian aliens from being deported. Congressman William Clay (D., MO) had charges in a civil suit against him dropped by the Justice Department in exchange for his agreement to repay overpayments for travel.

The Tongsun Park investigations of bribery involved still other congressmen. House Speaker Carl Albert (D., OK), John Brademas (D., IN), Edwin Edwards (D., LA), Richard Hanna (D., CA), Cornelius Gallagher (D., NJ), William Broomfield (R., MI), Otto Passman (D., LA), Joseph Addabo (D., NY), and Robert Leggett (D., CA) made headlines in the investigation for possible bribery in connection with the Korean businessman.

Congressman Hastings was charged with accepting kickbacks from staff members. At the Republican convention Reagan supporters were accused of attempting to "buy" two black Illinois delegates. In June of 1976 Elizabeth Ray (the *Washington Fringe Benefit*) became nationally known for her role in payroll fraud. Senator Joseph Montoya (D., NM), accused of being delinquent in tax payments in several earlier years, had been recommended for prosecution. His position as chair of the Senate Appropriations Subcommittee with jurisdiction over the Internal Revenue Service may have had an impact on the decision not to investigate further.

Another important change in the tone of Senate campaigns was the emergence of well-financed conservative political organizations friendly to Republican candidates, but working outside the Republican party. In 1972 national conservative organizations raised $250,000 for congressional campaigns. By October of 1976 they had raised an estimated $3.5 million.[2]

Defining the Incumbent's Image

Producer Neil South is the president of his own consulting firm located in the heart of Sunstate. After serving a short stint in Washington, D.C. as a press secretary, he returned to Sunstate, where he worked for several commercial advertising agencies. Neil likes politics, and it wasn't long before he ventured out on his own. He is active in every level of campaign in Sunstate, from races for governor and senator to local contests for the state legislature. As his reputation has grown, he has picked up races outside the state as well. In 1982, while handling Senator Cloistered's campaign for re-election, he also handled another Senate primary campaign in an adjoining state, a congressional race in the state, and nine local races. In defining the incumbent's image, South sees two critical elements.[3]

> We had two concepts that we felt needed to be sold to the people of Sunstate. People in Sunstate need to feel comfortable about the candidate, that he will do the right thing; and they need to feel that he won't be an embarrassment. They need confidence in his ability. Going in we had poll data that said people were confident but didn't feel very comfortable about him. We wanted to reinforce the confidence in him and develop that feeling of comfort with him. The reasons they weren't comfortable was that he has a national agenda, he tends to be very strident. The research shows that people thought he was arrogant. It was really clear. . . .

Much of the dialogue of the 1982 race between Senator Cloistered and Thomas Popular reverberated with the themes of the national political climate, despite the fact that both used local producers. How is it that a senator who had already demonstrated his formidable campaign skills was perceived as vulnerable? How is it that he went on to defeat an opponent who was widely acknowledged to be more person-

ally appealing? Prior to the 1982 campaign Senator Cloistered used public opinion polling to assess his strengths
and weaknesses. His producer, Neil South, describes his image thus:

> [Senator Cloistered is seen as] . . . very cold, I mean imper-
> sonal. Certainly arrogant, certainly aloof. But he is also per-
> ceived as very intelligent, and very powerful, particularly
> since the election. He was very dogmatic, ultraconserva-
> tive, and rather narrow minded. Early in his first term he
> changed some of that. I believe that he is a senator for all the
> people. . . . He has tried to be very fair, much more tolerant,
> much more open-minded. After the first couple of years he
> really mellowed. He's more patient. He still has his dogmatic
> issues. Abortion. He'll never give up on that. He should po-
> litically, morally he shouldn't. He's still evolving.

Given a candidate with this image—cold, arrogant, aloof,
dogmatic, and narrow-minded—how does a producer counter these perceptions? How could a candidate with this
image soundly defeat an opponent widely acknowledged to
be "a mountain climber, good-looking, a friend of [a movie
star]?"

What the incumbent Senator Dan Cloistered learned in
1976 is that the national climate, in part, shapes state races.
He used national mistrust of political leaders to trounce the
incumbent in 1976. He effectively played to a new national
climate in 1982, to keep his position in the U.S. Senate
secure.

What were the national perceptions that hurt the Democratic challenger? In part, Neil South sees the perceived image of the national Democratic party as having hurt the
opponent (Thomas Popular) and helped the incumbent Republican. The political culture of Sunstate was an important
factor in the videostyles of both candidates, since national
economic factors were clearly a hindrance to the Republi-

cans. Neil South interprets the outcome of the 1982 races thus.

> In the [1982] congressional races the Republicans took a beating. People attributed a slump in the economy—unemployment, to Reagan. People were made to feel insecure. In Sunstate the unemployment statistics were high but not as high as they were nationally. The issue was the voters really sustaining widely held conservative political beliefs. In Sunstate the issues just haven't been with the Democrats. Daniel's opponent was not for abortion, ERA, or gun control. But he was associated with the position of the national Democratic party on these issues.

According to South, the challenger was faced with the formidable task of disassociating himself from the national Democratic party at the same time he was trying to build statewide recognition. In a conservative state, the issues were with his conservative opponent. The challenger faced the problem of being a "me too" candidate. His personal appeal, acknowledged by all campaign participants, was the challenger's strength. But the incumbent was clearly able to counter that strength. The incumbent was also able to prevent the challenger from usurping public values in the presentation of his campaign message.

A Strategy for Reelection

Neil South minces no words in assessing the weaknesses of the incumbent. His ability to view both the incumbent and his challenger in hard terms contributes to his success at developing campaign strategy. South refuses to take sole credit for the strategic planning of the campaign, calling it a collaborative effort. His influence, however, looms large and is readily apparent when the ads themselves are viewed. Be-

fore examining the content of the spots, let us listen to Neil
South explain the strategy behind them.

We didn't write the strategy or participate in strategy development as much as we like to. Our advertising strategy we recommended to them. We took part of their strategy and our
recommendations and worked together on it.

. . . When his opponent announced, the polls showed a
horse race, dead even. His opponent was ahead with women
by 10 percent. He's a mountain climber, good-looking, a
friend of [movie star].

We went on the air earlier than any other campaign in Sunstate. We wanted to show a different side of Daniel. A side
that people had never seen before. The campaign nicknamed
two ads "hearts and flowers." They didn't talk about issues,
didn't give any reasons to vote for Daniel. No makeup, no
script. They have candid shots, really pretty pictures. We
tried to present Daniel as a dedicated family man—a warm,
caring, human being. We had thirty to forty hours on audio-
tape. We interviewed him late at night and got some nice
tender moments. Late at night he gets reflective. If you just
listened to the ad it makes no sense. It's just excerpts from
the audiotape. But it all flows.

In April/May we did the first flight. The first flight was
two two-minute spots, the hearts and flowers. Then we took
a poll and Daniel led by ten points. That's a twenty point
change. And we had moved women. We occasionally saw
some slippage, and then we'd insert the ads.

. . . In phase two we found a good formula so we didn't
want to change it. It was dedicated to reinforcing the confidence thing. But we didn't talk about pocketbook issues, we
talked about people issues. Four ads were produced, three
were aired. One was never aired. . . . One was home health
care. The other was crime, and the other one was nuclear
testing. All of those were that same style. Semidocumentary,
with real people, no makeup, no scripts. The home health
care and nuclear testing were real people. The crime spot

was an interview with a police chief. The old people were really hard to do—we had to go out and find some. Most of them are in pretty bad shape, so it took awhile to find one well enough to film.

The strategic emphasis of the campaign is softening negative public perceptions of Senator Cloistered's personal character. The focus is always on values—especially in the visual imagery. The audio message is less important in South's discussion of the campaign, than the *way* issues are talked about and dramatized. More than any other campaign studied here, this race epitomizes the philosophy of "showing, not telling." The visual character of television is maximized in the candidate's presentation of self.

The Incumbent's Message

The ads Neil South nicknamed "hearts and flowers" are indeed persuasive. The visual images seem to reveal the gentle, private side of Senator Cloistered's character. He is shown dressed in slacks and pullover sweater, making popcorn in the kitchen with his family, holding a child in his lap. The shots always include other people—he is never alone. The other people are always physically close to him. There is a preponderance of close-ups. Watching the spots places the viewer beside the senator, observing like some democratic guardian angel. The audio part of the ads reinforces this sensation as the viewer becomes privy to the senator's thoughts. It is a stream of consciousness sensation. The senator is a man with a dream, struggling in the pursuit of it.

> I never dreamed of the difficulties of being a U.S. senator. Because sometimes you're just not sure. What is the best approach? Nobody can have all the answers, and I certainly

don't claim to have them. Being a senator is a very difficult thing. But it's also a very rewarding thing. You feel like
you're helping the people of your state. I believe in the future
of all children. And I'm going to insure for all children, including my own, that there's a future like there was for me.

Our future of this county depends upon the education of
our children. I see in our young people more desire to learn,
and more desire to progress, and more desire to contribute. I
might add that they are reflective today. We have exceptional
young people.

There is no trace of arrogance in the musings of Dan
Cloistered. His voice is calm, thoughtful. There is no hint of
narrow-mindedness. Only a sincere quest for the right answers, for truth. There is no shadow of cold impersonality,
dogmatic injustice, over the way this man does his job. There
is only the aura of dedication, of a genuine affection for the
people whom he seeks to "help," and a commitment to family
and children. Not just his own family and children, but all
families of Sunstate. Little wonder that the ads were so effective in tempering the negative aspects of Senator Cloistered's
personal image going into the 1982 campaign.

The ads reflect Neil South's theory of how voters evaluate
candidates. Voters are ambivalent. Ads are intrusive. The
goal of the ad must therefore be to reduce ambivalence in a
nonintrusive way, to make an emotional impact and to create a believable identification. Neil South's understanding of
the essential character of the state is reflected in the way he
sees voters making their choices.

In Sunstate . . . well I think in general there's a real ambivalence to candidates. Every once in a while someone exciting
comes along. They [voters] dislike elections, dislike politicians, mistrust them. Ads are intrusive. We come right into
their homes, their cars, and practically throw-up in their
faces with all this stuff they don't really like, don't care about.

> I think voters don't like politics. In the later part of the campaign some do need information and look to ads. It's an emotional decision rather than a logical one for the most part.
>
> In Sunstate its very, very important to be able to discuss the issues intelligently but in street language. In Sunstate people like a common person. They want a politician like them, who thinks like they do, who votes like they do. They don't like arrogance. They don't like a guy who runs around jumping up and down taking credit for things. They look for balance. Even though they are conservative in their thinking they don't want right-wing crazies.

South has emphasized the importance to the candidate's popularity of personal attractiveness (in terms of personality characteristics rather than personal appearance), of similarity to the voters in terms of a way of thinking and talking, and of general conservative values. The role of reciprocity is not explicit in South's view of how voters choose between two candidates, but it comes through in the casework spots he produced. He does see the decision as an emotional one, sees the voter's choice as an emotional commitment rather than a logical calculation.

The incumbent, Daniel Cloistered, takes a somewhat different view of what the voters are looking for. In the senator's view, the past record is less relevant than future promise. The senator indicates less regard for intimacy than for issue information. He is, however, cognizant that simply taking issue stands is not enough. The senator believes it is the shared history between candidate and constituency, as well as the future prospects, which are decisive.

> Generally I think [what the voters are looking for] is sincerity, personal appearance, ability to articulate your position, warmth, and friendship which goes along with sincerity. For both the incumbent and the challenger, what they promise for the future is more important than the record.
>
> If you're talking about TV you can put together clever ads

that appeal to anybody. Some people can; I don't subscribe
to that approach. I think there are other things.

Again, the importance of personal attractiveness is stated
in terms of personality characteristics rather than physical
appearance. Unlike other incumbents interviewed in previous chapters, Senator Cloistered sees his record as less
important than what he can promise. This perception may
be uniquely the result of his political situation in Sunstate
in 1982—he was not effectively challenged to explain his
record. Thus he could concentrate his message on future
prospects.

What is the nature of the future promise that Dan Cloistered views as so critical to voters? The answer can be found
in examining a series of spots produced by Neil South for
the senator's campaign. Each of the spots focuses on a different issue—medical care for the elderly, nuclear testing, and
crime. A fourth spot blends these issues together, as a background for the senator's comments on what his job means
to him.

The first of these spots, on medical care for the elderly,
begins with shots of two women taking a third woman in a
wheelchair for a walk. The camera focuses on the same two
women fixing a meal and feeding the elderly woman in the
wheelchair. We see the younger of the two women playing the
piano while the wheelchair-bound older woman listens. The
camera cuts to shots of Senator Cloistered at work, talking
with his staff, examining papers, at a committee hearing.
There is no background music in this spot. We hear only the
slowly spoken words of one of the women. There is a poi-
gnancy in the spot, a heaviness of heart. The woman's words
echo through each shot.

My mother requires constant medical attention. We wanted
her at home rather than having her in a care center. But
medicare just would not pay for many necessities, even though

it cost less to have her at home. . . . My mother definitely has a real feeling that she belongs. She knows she has her relatives around her. . . .

[The voice of Senator Cloistered intervenes.] . . . Our aged people worked hard all their lives so that we could have better lives. So we're encouraging their children to bring them into their homes and to be more family-oriented. . . .

The crime spot creates a different kind of tension from the spot just described. It is night. The viewer is on patrol with a policeman. The radio breaks the stillness: "All units be advised, report of a burglary in progress. . . ." A second voice breaks in:

It's a very frustrating thing for an officer to work the long hours that they do, apprehend a criminal, and then find that same criminal back on the street, committing the same types of crime, time after time after time. . . . When you make a conviction, the man finally is sentenced, he's put on probation or parole and he's back on the streets. It's not fair to the officers. Not fair to the taxpayers. And it's not fair to those victims.

The spot creates apprehension. A sense that something is about to happen. This is mixed with frustration. Mingled with the frustration of the police officer is the frustration of the senator in his fight to toughen the criminal justice system. The spot ends with a black-and-white still photo of the senator in his office.[4] As justice is black and white. As the fight goes on. He is still working.

The spot which synthesizes the three issue-focused spots serves to reinforce the earlier images and provides a context for Senator Cloistered to talk about what it means to be a senator. Visually, we meet again the woman from the nuclear testing spot. She is looking at photographs. The camera cuts to the image of the woman playing the piano for the elderly, wheelchair bound woman. The camera cuts to the police chief standing with two officers ready to go out on patrol.

The audio portion of the ad is dominated by the voice of Senator Cloistered. It is an out-take of the hours of audio-tape made late at night with the senator philosophizing.

> . . . I kind of look at this job as one that, that's what I'm here for. To work with individual Sunstaters and solve their problems and, of course, help them in any way I can. You know you couldn't help but be excited by that. You know you're helping people that really need your help, but that can't help themselves. And I think, what greater work can I do? Now we're not always successful, but we do try. And I intend to continue to do that. . . .

The last set of ads produced for the Cloistered campaign is more overt in placing the senator in direct confrontation with his audience. All of the ads discussed thus far showed the senator working with people, without asking for anything in return. In many of them, individuals themselves spoke out on behalf of the senator, or in response to problems. However two spots are real campaign-trail pitches for support. These two spots feature the senator introducing himself and asking the audience for their votes. They are short and simple, and lack the visual appeal and evocative quality of the earlier spots. The message: "stay the course."

> I'm Daniel Cloistered. You know, in 1980 America turned a corner. The changes that President Reagan began, which I'm proud to have had a small part in, have set a totally new course. That's why this Senate election, this year, in Sunstate, is *more than a popularity contest*. We have to determine whether we're going to continue in a new direction or whether we're going to return to the old tax, spend, and promise politics of the past. I believe the changes are good and are starting to work. If you agree, I'd like your vote on election day.

I'm Daniel Cloistered. The issues we're dealing with right now in the Senate are family issues. They hit us at home right where we live. We've cut inflation dramatically and of course that prevents our paychecks from being gobbled up so quickly. Interest rates are coming down too, and that helps every family, especially younger families. Of course, our problems aren't over, but instead of tax, spend, and promise policies of the past, we're offering hope for the future— for every family. Throughout Sunstate and throughout all America. [Emphasis added.]

These two spots are particularly fascinating because Senator Cloistered is able to subtly take Thomas Popular's biggest asset (his popularity) and make it a negative. Furthermore, his own philosophy that future promise is most important is contradicted. He says, in fact, that he wants to end the "politics of promises"—and follows that by saying that he offers "hope for the future." Senator Cloistered is not running against Thomas Popular, he is running against thirty years of Democratic control of the Senate—a control that ended in 1980 when the Republicans won a majority. What better opponent to choose to run against than one you have already beaten?

In describing the senator's constituency Neil South emphasizes the Sunstate mentality and how that mentality is linked to elements of the local culture. Neil sees the state as very, very individual in its thinking, conservative socially and fiscally, and independent. In his words, "you do *not* tell Sunstaters what to do. . . . The Sunstate mentality is we can do it ourselves." It is clear that Neil and the incumbent senator for whom he produced the ads had divergent views of the campaign, both in terms of what was presented to voters and the process by which the voter/viewer came to support the senator. The senator, for example, refers disparagingly to producing "clever ads that appeal to anybody." Neil South, on the other hand, sees the necessity for overcoming an initial negative reaction to politics (which may best be accomplished through clever ads). Neil South's focus is countering the negative perceptions of the senator that existed going into the campaign with an unrelenting positive flow of personal information ("pretty pictures" and "tender moments"). The senator's view emphasizes drawing contrasts—attacking his opponent's record or the opposition party's record.

Several basic political rules are followed. In particular, the senator used surrogates to respond to attacks from his challenger. He was also able to define his challenger's image, at least in part, by associating him with the national Democratic party and its liberal causes.

> A person's record is important to attack. In my case the other person couldn't attack because in most cases they agreed with it, and when they didn't they were afraid most of the citizens of Sunstate agreed with it.
>
> In 1976 my opponent was a liberal. That was easy to attack. People could see what he hadn't done in the past.
>
> I fought for the balanced budget. . . . He [Thomas Popular] finally wound up attacking Reagan. People knew that a conservative Cloistered wouldn't outspend a moderate Popular.
>
> The theme of our campaign was "you need to support Ronald Reagan and stay the course. You can't turn around the country in two years. If the Democrats gain more control you won't be able to change, to progress. It would be better to continue." Interest rates were down, we were starting to pull the country out of the mess. The best way to control this was to stay the course.
>
> . . . We ignored most of them [attacks]. Responses were mainly by other people who were credible. We felt most of the attacks were not credible; they were ridiculous. We didn't have to respond to charges that I was a big-spending conservative. Nobody believed it. Generally, if we had vicious stuff we had other people answer it. . . . The only thing was a debate. I was getting pretty tired of the same old dribble. I got pretty vociferous. And the press blew it all out of proportion.

But we were able to turn that around too. We sent out 14,000 pieces of direct mail, and I didn't back down from my comments at all. Not one bit . . .

Senator Cloistered's approach to answering the attacks of the challenger was vastly different from (and much more effective than) the approach used by Harold Doright. Where Doright directly and personally answered the attacks of Johnny Fasttrack, Daniel Cloistered, like Matt Niceguy, used credible surrogates, keeping himself at an appropriately senatorial distance from the fray.

While local producer Neil South produced most of the advertising for Senator Cloistered, a Washington-based consultant did produce several attack spots for the senator. These were aired very little during the campaign. Neil South was sharply critical of the ads produced by the Washington firm.

> We didn't have to respond. The last month of the campaign the pollster said it's over. No way Popular can win. There was no need to respond to negative criticism. Scam Priestly was brought in. Two ads were aired. Daniel on camera talking philosophically about working with the president.
>
> Since we intrude into people's homes with advertising there is no reason we have to give them awful advertising. Putting Daniel on camera in front of a mike was contrary to everything we had tried to do early on. It's contrary to everything we know about good advertising. I think the ads Priestly did showed Daniel at his worst. I don't think people were interested. Political advertising can be creative. *It must follow, it has to follow, all the rules of good advertising.* [Emphasis added.]

The incumbent's message is carefully crafted to culminate in an intimate connection with his constituents. The role of issue information is not ignored—rather issues are talked about in a way that enhances the degree of comfort that voter/viewers feel with the senator. The audio content of the senator's presentation of self either gives access to the senator's most private thoughts or testifies to the senator's reciprocity toward fellow constituents with whom we empathize.

The visual aspects of Senator Cloistered's presentation of self reflect the importance the producer places on building intimacy between candidate and viewer. To counter perceptions that Cloistered is cool, he is shown in physical proximity to family members—holding a child, reaching out to touch a shoulder, to feed a dog. To counter perceptions that he is distant (has a national agenda), most shots are of him back in Sunstate.

Although the senator is certainly physically attractive, his presentation of self in no way makes the race a beauty contest. Personality attractiveness is emphasized much more than personal appearance. Similarity to the constituency is conveyed through showing agreement on mainstream traditional values. Each element of the senator's videostyle thus makes the case that there can be no more desirable alternative in all of Sunstate.

Controlling the Message

Neil South and Senator Cloistered agreed over the extent to which the senator controlled his media message. According to South,

> Daniel had very little, if any control. He was always consulted. But in terms of message and content, he had little control. The campaign manager had complete control. The ad agency had little control. I think that for the most part candidates tend to be too emotional about winning, and so they aren't the best person to make media decisions. For the most part candidates are too close to make wise decisions about actual media.

In the senator's view: "The campaign manager had complete control over the campaign. I don't recall overruling him at any time. He had a free hand, knew what he was doing. I never saw him flustered; he's very calm."

Why did the senator relinquish so much control over his presentation of self? We hypothesized in chapter 4 that candidates might be more willing to concede the visual aspects of their videostyles. We reiterate that hypothesis and add two more: Candidates will relinquish the most control over their videostyles: 1) in decisions of visual content or production technique, and 2) in races when there is no need for strategic shifts over the course of the campaign. Incumbents, because of the already great burdens on their time, are more amenable to delegating control than are challengers.

Analyzing Defeat

For the incumbent, the race began with the question of continuation or deterioration of his relationship with his constituents looming large. At issue were some fairly prevalent negative perceptions of the senator in terms of his personal attractiveness, and less so his similarity to his constituents. The threat to the incumbent was a situation ripe for the appearance of a more desirable alternative—as which Popular hoped to be perceived. The incumbent addressed his vulnerability through a presentation of self in his advertising that softened his personal appeal, while at the same time he embraced local conservative values on some key issues. An integral part of his message was reciprocity to constituents shown in the casework testimonials.

The opening presented by the incumbent's negative personal image was recognized by the challenger and his producer. What they did not anticipate was that they would need to respond to the incumbent's ability to present himself in a way that countered those negative perceptions. In effect, the challenger lost his voice for much of the campaign, since he was unable to come up with a response that convinced people he was still the more desirable alternative or raised doubts about the credibility of the "new" Senator Cloistered.

While Neil South first introduced the notion of an intimacy factor, it was Thomas Popular, the candidate he helped defeat, who stressed its importance in the outcome of the race. According to Popular:

> Most voters vote out of their gut, and not out of their head. There's a "comfort factor." My analysis of voters is that they tend to pick the person that when they go out to vote they say "hmm, who makes me more comfortable." And then they pick that person. I get higher ratings than Daniel in job ratings, so how could I lose an election to him? They were uncomfortable about me going to Washington and being another economic liberal. They knew Daniel would be a better friend to the president than I would be. Daniel did a good job, a very effective job, of being more personable. They call him "dull Daniel" through the media, and I'm convinced that someone on his staff grabbed him and told him "you've got to stop being so arrogant."

Challenger Tom Popular and his producer, Bud Smart, agree with Neil South's assessment of the race. Smart further views the incumbent President Reagan as an important influence in boosting Senator Cloistered's campaign.

> Here's a guy [Reagan] who in 1980 got a large share of the popular vote. He came here twice in 1982. People in Sunstate still loved him. He came to town the weekend before the election and had already been here in August. He filled the [convention center] and we were buried. It just reversed any momentum we may have had—[Reagan] campaigning for Cloistered. People just said that they were willing to give the

president's program more time. There's this local political
thing that "we've come [this far], made the great sacrifice,
and built Sunstate." They were willing to do it again. It's part
of the political norm."

Thomas Popular also acknowledges the strength of the
Reagan magnet in the 1982 campaign. He sees that the void
in his own campaign was intensified by Reagan's larger-
than-life political presence in the state. The incumbent's
message was simple, and explicitly linked to the popular
president. His own campaign did not respond with a reason
for abandoning the incumbent (who had shown himself to
be a good and faithful suitor), the president, or the president's program (which was not yet working). Thomas Popular reflects on the race:

> Well, first of all I didn't take it very personally [the 1982 de-
> feat]. I didn't blame myself for losing. There were forces at
> work in our conservative state that my opponent was good at
> seizing on and exploiting. We were riding a Reagan train in
> 1982. He [Daniel Cloistered] was running around saying, "Do
> you want to give Reagan a chance to succeed?" I felt I never
> had a chance to answer to that in my campaign. *I never had
> a reason for people to vote for me.* The best campaign man-
> ager is timing. If I'd been running in Outland I'd have felt
> bad if I hadn't won. But in Sunstate I had an excuse. It's a
> conservative state. [Emphasis added.]
> I think there's no clear path to office. Our initial polling
> showed me pretty popular vis à vis Daniel. It started out as a
> personality thing. But the more we got into it, the issues,
> the less we had to say. We started out trying to be everything
> Daniel was. It was like running around saying, "Vote for me,
> I'll be a friend to the president too." About Labor Day we
> started taking the president on. We declared his program a
> failure and took it head on.
> I felt that I had something to offer that Daniel didn't. I felt
> that there was a lot of unfairness in the country. The party

told me that I was the only one who could win. There were some leadership things that needed to be done. The tax program was unfair. But the irony was, we didn't run on that in the beginning.

In any campaign there are thousands of potential turning points and myriad ways in which to snatch defeat from the jaws of victory. If one were to pinpoint a single reason for the defeat of Thomas Popular, it would surely be the strategic decisions made around Labor Day in defining his image. Why pit himself against the popular president instead of the relatively unpopular incumbent? Reagan's popularity in the state did slip a little as unemployment rates went up, however, unemployment in Sunstate was below the national average.[5] Popular let the focus of the campaign slip from his strength (personal character) when the incumbent made himself more personally appealing. His fallback strategy was to emphasize issues—however, the incumbent's issue values were more similar to the average Sunstater than Popular's issue positions. Thomas Popular did not set out to lose. Yet every step of the way the incumbent was able to manipulate the political agenda to Popular's disadvantage. This becomes even clearer when Popular's producer discusses strategy. Neil South's focus was on building positives. Bud Smart's orientation is preventing mishaps:[6]

I was called in [to the campaign] in February or March, and really nothing was done until much later. Our overall strategy was to make sure that, number one, Tom was never embarrassed.

[By that I mean] that he didn't ever get put in the position of saying something, particularly in the media, that he didn't mean. To make sure that he was never physically or intellectually embarrassed.

The governor's ad (for Popular) was courageous. Sunstaters don't like confrontation. It upsets them. And here was the governor going into their homes night after night and telling them, "hey this guy's no good." It made the public aware of the problem, but it ended up being sixes. It nearly doubled Tom's negative rating. He started out at 14 percent, and ended up pushing 35 percent.

Every piece was aimed at Everyman. That's exactly the way we were trying to buy it, for Everyman. What we were trying to express is: "you've got a guy in there who's never home, doesn't know what's going on. And you have a chance to elect a guy who's from here, understands the problems, and cares."

Assessments of what went on in the race in Sunstate produce the greatest agreement among all the campaign principals—incumbent, challenger, and producers—that we have seen. Reagan and his coattail are perceived by all as significant factors, and all acknowledge that the reputation of the national Democratic party rubbed off on this moderate Democrat, hurting him in a conservative state. Popular acknowledges that the incumbent was able to control the campaign agenda. All of the campaign principals agree that issue similarity helped the incumbent because he was also able to improve his intimate connection with constituents.

How Do Voters Evaluate Candidates?

Perceptions of just what voters look for, and how they go about evaluating information, are closest between the producer for the incumbent (Neil South) and the man he helped defeat (Thomas Popular). Both mention the importance of intimate connection between voters and candidates. Tom Popular specifically refers to a "comfort factor."

. . . [in terms of my own image] warmth was high. People felt good about me as a person, that I could be trusted. Dan was low on trust, many people kept calling him arrogant, cocky—

they still do—it's not as though he's changed his image completely. Cold, the coldness/warmness towards him tipped cold.

Early pollsters felt quite positive about a win. It looked like 46 percent to 43 percent for months on end. I never got closer than those initial polls. *I think the reason it was a locked race was I never found anything to say that would convince them I should be a senator.*

. . . [in terms of issues] Sunstaters consider any Democrat in office in this state to be a conservative, or you wouldn't be in office. Someone they could be comfortable with on issues. *What does he really have to offer in Washington? That's a good question, one we didn't answer.*

I think [the voters] thought I didn't have enough whiskers—you know, my relative youth. And my style as a conciliator rather than a yeller may have given my image a certain softness. The issues just didn't cut that deep. *Dan had a simple message, "stay the course." I didn't have an equitable simple message.* [Emphasis added.]

Bud Smart shares many of the sentiments of Tom Popular. Smart started with the campaign as a media buyer. When the consultant originally hired had problems meeting delivery schedules, Smart took over all media responsibilities. He and Popular are long-time friends. As a resident of Sunstate, Smart is sensitive to the local political culture and norms. Unlike the race in Outland examined in chapter 4—which pitted an out-of-state producer against a local producer—the race in Sunstate pitted two local consultants against each other. This factor may also help account for the level of agreement one sees in the analyses of the race. The people interviewed all know one another and have been a part of the political history of the state.

According to Smart, there is no single process by which the voter decides. It is more of a filtering process—with each individual sifting through the information present, selecting bits and pieces. The notion of individuals a priori setting up criteria and using these criteria as standards by which they evaluate candidates is foreign to him.

> I really think it ends up being an individual thing for each race. They just choose little bits and pieces from what's presented to them. They just don't set up criteria.
>
> Excuse me for saying this, but it was like a junior high school election. Our guy was more popular, better looking, and he talked nicer. Had we gone out and outdone Dan in that area we would probably have done better than we did. Dan was a nice guy who the public viewed as competent, and *there wasn't any reason to vote against him.* We lost the election on the issues because we didn't choose an issue until October and it was way too late. [Emphasis added.]
>
> Dan chose the issue. Chose the national slogan, "Stay the Course," and never varied from it. At the same time he did a little bit to make himself more loveable. In April and May he was running two minute spots purporting to be a concerned family man, citizen of Sunstate and the United States, a tough but respected member of the Senate. At that time we didn't have the money to go on the air, so we calculated that the only thing we could do was try for a lot of free press and hang on to our money for the fall.
>
> The second week of October we had a big meeting. Tommy [Popular] said I'm tired of not having anything to say. The issue will be the economy. Unemployment figures were just coming out, and Tom hit the stump with that issue. The only reason he chose that was that not only was it a national issue, but Tom is an economist. We were closing in on the national level of unemployment, but never hit double digit. We pushed maybe 9.6.
>
> Social security seemed to be an issue. Everybody was making something out of it. In my view, the elderly walked out [of the voting booth] saying, "I hope I'm doing the right thing. Am I going to do as my beloved President asked me to do"—who essentially comes down and says, "you have nothing to fear," and, "I'll take care of this." Or, "am I going to vote for Popular"—who says, "if somebody with some guts

doesn't go up there and do something you're not going to get any."

[In terms of Tom's image] we were trying to say that he is intelligent and that he cares about the state, and its people. That he is tough enough to do something. On the negative side, we perceived in the early polling that Tom is not "senatorial." That he isn't intelligent enough on the national issues to represent a Sunstate position. The single thing with Tom was that you can trust him. People view him as honest and straightforward, hardworking, and that he is a Sunstater. Tom was born and raised in Sunstate. Cloistered moved in, from out of nowhere, no one knows where he moved in from, and got himself elected to work on his national agenda.

In terms of strategy, the producer for challenger Tom Popular sounds much like the incumbent Senator Cloistered. Both focus on the need for building expectations of the future. While Senator Cloistered emphasizes that "what you promise for the future is more important than past performance," he also acknowledges the importance of attacking the record. Bud Smart sees the "promise" for the future as the basis of the entire campaign.

We had weekly polls, 250 every week with every third week doubled [500]. When Tom decided what the issue was going to be, the next week they fired the pollster, and we didn't hire another one. This was in mid-October. So I don't know exactly what the effect was, but I think it polarized the voters and ultimately was probably the thing that solidified the Republicans who probably were going to vote for Tom.

[Senator Cloistered's attacks on Tom] . . . were typical underground political activity that goes on in the state. He [Cloistered] ignored him [Tom]. Cloistered acted as if Tom didn't exist. He referred to him as "Mr. Popular," never by his title. There was a telephone campaign that went on early [July]. Under the guise of doing a poll they would make a call and say, "would you vote for anybody that supports the ERA?

Did you know that Tom Popular supports the language of the ERA? We were called twice. My wife was called and I was called. It was really slanted, and in some cases they found a way to make totally unfounded claims about Tom.

Tom kept demanding publicly a debate. And he made the debate an issue. We didn't debate prior to Labor Day, which was what Tom was trying to force. The debates were the grandest moments of the campaign. They [the candidates] had to say what they really meant, what they knew. Tom was 60–40. There were five major debates. Tom so trashed Dan on the third or fourth debate. But there wasn't a large audience. He caught the senator in an out-and-out lie. Tom had a headline from the paper and showed it to him on the air, of Dan saying something different. It was on a social security vote I think. Afterward Dan went up to one of his aides and grabbed him by the tie and threatened him. He was shaking his finger in his face.

On TV alone we spent nearly $500,000, another $150,000 for production. We made nineteen ads, and three never ran. There was one that I didn't want to run. By the time Tom approved it, it had no effect. We didn't get it on the air until the last week of the campaign. It was one of those emotion spots that you've got to see a couple of times to know what he's saying. I thought it was chickenshit. . . . There was a spot that had people joining the Popular campaign. It only ran the last two days. The guy I was working with loved it. At the end the screen just went dark for a few seconds. He [the guy worked with] said it would show people that if they ever wanted to see Tom Popular again they'd have to vote for him.

There were three others out of the "chickenshit session." Another "heart on the sleeve" thing, but this time he was talking about [things like] "every American has a right to freedom from poverty." Then there was an economy one and economy two spot, where Tom talked about the economy. The things he understood.

[Overall, what went wrong was] *we had a campaign without a promise, and if you have a campaign without a promise, you haven't got a campaign.* [Emphasis added.]

The Challenger's Message

In person, Tom Popular exudes warmth and charm. He has a ready smile, a firm handshake, and an easy manner. Very little of this personal appeal, and none of his good humor, shows through in the television spots. The spots are short—generally no more than thirty seconds. Visually, the spots tend to show him in semiformal campaign situations, such as speaking before a small group, as opposed to talking with people one on one. The lack of a clear, simple message—pointed to by both Popular and Smart—is also apparent in the ads. Furthermore, the sequence of airing the spots is disjointed. There is no buildup to intimate connection—one cannot judge where the relationship is by viewing the spots.

A spot on the elderly begins with a medium shot of Popular talking to a group of old people. He is wearing a light grey suit. He looks a little swarthy. His heavy beard shows clearly on camera, despite the fact that he has recently shaved. The camera moves back to a medium shot of an old man talking to Popular. The spot ends with a still photo of Popular framed by the slogan "Popular for Senate."

The audio portion of the spot begins with an excerpt from Popular's speech: "It really makes me angry that in this country we're continually putting people second." A strong masculine voice cuts in "Dan Cloistered voted against meals on wheels, against social security—and for Sunstate, that's just not right." The voice of the old man is heard next, cracking as he says, " . . . and put it in a little milk carton to take home to have something to eat for supper at night. Those people's not wasting anything, and it's a sin to take it away from them." The voice of the male announcer interjects again "Tom Popular; [pause] he'll put Sunstate first."

A "jobs" spot follows much the same format. The camera scans a mountainside to settle on a small group of people surrounding Popular. The camera focuses on Popular as he speaks, moving from a close-up to a medium shot. There is a close-up of a young man in the group. Another close-up of Popular. The camera moves back for a reaction shot of Popular while the young man speaks. The spot ends with the same still photo of Popular framed by the slogan "Popular for Senate."

The audio portion of the ad features Popular talking with a group of miners. Popular states, "Right now the Department of Commerce is not limiting the illegal imports of copper from abroad. These are clear violations. . . ." A woman interjects, "How can they get away with it?" A male announcer cuts in, "The issue in this campaign is this. Has Daniel Cloistered done everything possible to protect Sunstate jobs and industry? A commitment in Washington to work for Sunstate jobs, that's putting Sunstate first." One of the men standing around in the group with Popular says, "We'd like to see someone in there who will represent the people and not the money." The announcer's voice breaks in again, "And that's Tom Popular for U.S. Senate."

An "accomplishments" spot closely resembles a spot produced in Outland, by a different producer, for incumbent Hal Doright. It consists of a collage of cuts of Tom Popular going about a very busy day while an announcer reads a laundry list of Popular's accomplishments as a public servant. While the spot conveys a certain authoritative air by virtue of the specific factual information contained, it fails to create a sense that the viewer *knows* Tom Popular. The sense of "knowing" is what Cloistered's ads create so well. What others have referred to as a "comfort factor" is creating an atmosphere in which viewers feel that they know the candidate intimately at the end of the two-minute or thirty-second spot.

Thirty-second intimacy may sound like a contradiction in terms. But it is not. People make judgments about other people in less time than that *routinely* in their daily lives. These first impressions, or judgments, are hard to erase once formed. What Cloistered was able to do was provide viewers with that sense of closeness, of knowing him "as a man," of knowing the quality of his character. Factual information can be more superficial than this deeper way of knowing. Facts about how many jobs have been brought to the state do not necessarily allow one to have confidence in the future. Knowing the quality of a man's character in this deeper sense allows one to have confidence in expectations for the future.

Message Control

Both Bud Smart and Tom Popular agree that it was Popular who exercised control over the campaign and the messages presented through the spots. Final decisions on what would air, and when, belonged to the candidate. Both also acknowledge that the role the candidate played in the day-to-day campaign operations probably hurt both the candidate (exhausting him) and the campaign (since he could not be objective). According to Bud Smart,

> . . . [Tom] made the final decision. I'm sure that there are times when Tom would rather not make those decisions, but all that material in the final analysis represents him. He exercised total control over all his scheduling, and he had definite ideas of where he was going and where he wasn't going to go. He exercised, eventually, control over the ideas expressed. But coming in October it was too late.
>
> I would say that the one area where he might have done better was the volunteer effort. He wasn't watching the volunteer effort very well. The reason I say that is that it wasn't working as well as it should have. The level of participation wasn't nearly as high as it should be. The equipment at head-

quarters wasn't working as it should have. And no one was really screaming about it.

Popular also sees that the role he attempted to play in the campaign made the locus of responsibility for getting things done unclear. According to Popular,

> I tried to exercise pretty strong control, but I know some of it got away from me. I got in a couple of biffs with the campaign manager. I felt terrible about a spot I cut criticizing Dan, and the governor's spot ran too long. I'd be so busy I couldn't keep up with all of it. Someone would come up to me and say something about an ad, and I'd say "Why is that spot still on the air? Get it off." If you win, all those things are brilliant. If you lose, all those things are mistakes.

Perhaps the level of control Popular attempted to exercise over his campaign was another factor contributing to his defeat. The candidate must be the candidate. An attempt to play multiple roles in the campaign diverts attention from each role, scatters responsibility for accomplishing tasks, and in addition to exhausting the candidate, weakens his organization. Being informed about the campaign organization's functioning is highly desirable, but it is not the same as making every trivial and nontrivial decision. The candidates must set directions, exercise veto power, and allow others, whose professional judgment they trust, to carry out the operation.

Reflections on a Loss

Tom Popular accurately perceives the issue void in his campaign message. While his personal appearances may have relied on his charm and warmth as a means of winning the hearts and votes of Sunstate, his television advertising is void in this latter respect also. Popular acknowledges having made a conscious strategic decision to attempt to go with an issue message rather than communicating what kind of man he is.

> We started out with personality on our side and tried to go with issues instead. But we didn't really have an issue. Didn't have anything on our side. Unemployment was high. We hoped people would identify with us and try to get rid of the Reagan approach. But the voters attitude was, "hey, that's a legacy of the free-spending Democrats. We need to give Reagan a chance to let his program work."
>
> [If I had the race to run over again] . . . I would have been clearer on my opposition to the president and to Cloistered. *It was a mistake to try to beguile the voters with my personality and slip through the cracks.* We wouldn't have the convoluted strategy we started with. I'll never run a race again on personality. I don't think you can win that way. [Emphasis added.]

For the incumbent, Daniel Cloistered, the only regret seems to be that there was overkill. He perceives that in some areas the campaign made a greater effort than necessary. In hindsight, he would spend less, and spend it differently.

> I'd do more planning. Try to save more of the money we spent. On the other hand, we had one of the most sophisticated campaigns. Well organized. It was highly computerized. We did the best job on grass roots. There were tremendous resources being brought in to defeat me.
>
> I'd save money in some areas and spend it in others. We spent a lot on direct mail. We raised about $90,000 on direct mail and almost a third of it from Sunstate. Direct mail costs were tremendous and didn't pay off until the end of the campaign. I like the idea of little people contributing, and it helped.
>
> I think as far as spending, we spent the money wisely. We spent most on grass roots, and we did spend a lot on media. If I had some extra money I'd probably spend some more on

media and on people. Most of our people were volunteers, but we did have a well-organized staff. I'd have spent more on staff.

Conclusions

What conclusions can we draw from the reflections of the candidates and producers involved in this race? Issue information and basic facts about a candidate create the first level of knowing the candidate. This first level establishes a candidate's cue value and allows him to cross the "threshold of awareness."[7]

The public's cognition of a candidate is a necessary but insufficient condition for the development of the political relationship. Knowing his name, his face, basic facts about his career or issue identifications—these constitute the most superficial level of knowing the candidate. For political support to be expressed, candidates must create a deeper level of knowing. The "threshold of affection" must be crossed.

The "comfort factor" or "intimate connection" discussed by the candidates and producers of Sunstate are references to this deeper way of knowing the candidate. Intimacy is needed for the voter/viewer to catapult the candidate over the final hurdle to election.

The incumbent's successful production strategy used in Sunstate emphasized softening the initially negative perceptions of his character with positive information. The intimacy created by "tender moments" with, and "pretty pictures" of, the incumbent was not responded to by the challenger.

While the challenger accurately perceived the lack of a promise in his campaign message, his spots also failed to create a sense of the kind of man Tom Popular is. What went wrong for Tom Popular?

He chose to run against a popular incumbent president widely perceived in extremely favorable terms in Sunstate. He could have run against the incumbent senator exploiting some potentially lethal negative perceptions of the latter's character—if not his ability. Popular also failed to capitalize on his own innate warmth and personal charm, instead trying to give Sunstaters a reason to vote for him which was inconsistent with his true strengths as a candidate. On many levels he is not in agreement with the voters on the issues—and when he was, his own positions were overridden by his association with the national Democratic party.

These problems notwithstanding, the race still might have been won had Popular's campaign been more focused. It is harder to change an impression than to create one. Senator Cloistered obtained the electoral advantage early by defining his own image (showing viewers who he was as a man) in highly glowing terms. Television is a visual medium. Drama is important in getting viewers' attentions. Senator Cloistered's strategy was based on showing, rather than telling. Tom Popular resorted to telling—a strategic error.

Although both Popular and his producer Bud Smart were very sensitive to the local culture and political norms of Sunstate, the campaign agenda was defined very early by Cloistered and his staff. They effectively handed Popular the baggage of the national Democratic party, and he ended up carrying it through the campaign. The incumbent usurped local values for himself, at the same time making himself more personally appealing.

Finally, perhaps the most important lesson to be learned from this contest is that the burden of proof is always on the challenger. While highly personal strong attacks are a risky strategy, it is entirely appropriate for the challenger to raise questions about the incumbent's performance in office. Questions about the incumbent's relationship to his constituency are also appropriately raised. Even in raising questions and attacking, the candidate's behavior is analogous to a courtship. If there is any doubt about the appropriateness of a question, the candidate/producer must ask himself if the tactic would work romantically. A strident, angry suitor is generally unattractive, and unsuccessful.

Every state has different needs, and the first step is knowing what the courted public ultimately wants. What dreams lie unfulfilled in the hearts of potential constituents? There has to be a certain "chemistry" between a candidate and the voters. In the absence of chemistry, other things can work—in particular attentiveness, attentiveness, and attentiveness. After that, hard work, dependability, and shared values are important. Establishing this sort of presence in the state can create a chemistry.

The candidates are right in their assessment that "promises" for the future are important. For the incumbent, future promises are important for two reasons. First, all time spent painting a future is less time spent explaining the past. As noted in chapters 3 and 4, the challenge to defend the record can be the ruin of an incumbent simply because it is impossible not to offend someone over a term (or several terms) of office. Second, the future promise is important for incumbents because it makes more difficult the challenger's job of presenting himself as the more desirable alternative.

For the challenger, future promises are no less important but for different reasons. In most instances, challengers cannot evoke a shared past in courting constituents. Since past experience cannot help them establish bonds, they must rely on future promises. These promises also help them to persuade constituents of their greater desirability as alternatives to the incumbents they seek to replace. "A little bored with the representation that you're getting in Washington? Elect me for sustained excitement. Beginning to disagree with national policy? Elect me and your values will be expressed. Do you feel that promises have not been kept? Elect me and dreams will be fulfilled." The vividness with which a challenger can show what a future with him in office will be like is likely to be directly related to the extent to which he is perceived as a more desirable alternative to the incumbent.

6

Conclusions

This book has concentrated on creating a sense of the political styles of the candidates involved in three U.S. Senate races. A candidate's videostyle is different from interpersonal "home style" in several ways. First, videostyle is not determined solely by the candidate. Producers influence not only the content but also the form of presentation of self. In political advertising through television, the candidate need not be physically present in the ad for the viewer/voter to form or change impressions of him. The candidate's message is translated through the producer to the viewer. The interpersonal presentation of self relies on no such translator.

In home style, the presentation of self usually involves small, homogeneous audiences, slow message transmission, and emphasizes the candidate's ability to think on his feet. The presentation of self in videostyle involves large, heterogeneous audiences and rapid and simultaneous message transmission; it also emphasizes the candidate's and producer's abilities to anticipate audience reactions. While candidates generally exercise the right to veto certain "presentations of themselves," the spots that are aired are steeped in, and clearly reflect, the producer's philosophy.

Which "self" were the candidates attempting to project? How did they in fact succeed in projecting themselves? What led them in a particular strategic direction? The appropriateness of a particular presentation of self is dependent on the stage of the relationship between candidate and constituency. There are five stages, but not all candidates will pass through each stage. "Initial attraction" is most important for challengers and for incumbents in competitive situations. "Building a relationship" follows initial attraction and can be critical for both incumbents or challengers; it is the stage that builds familiarity and preference upon awareness. "Continuation" and "deterioration" are stages usually experienced by the candidates late in the campaign. They represent turning points in the political relationship and hinge on the kind and quality of future promises. "Ending" is a stage which half of the candidates in any election year will endure.

Candidates and producers do in fact have theories about what voters are looking for and how they make voting decisions. These theories loosely resemble the ideas of social scientists and influence the candidates' videostyle. Candidates' and producers' theories about how electoral outcomes are determined revolve around the distillation of two key factors—information and intimacy. Both factors are important at all stages of the relationship with varying degrees of emphasis. However, giving the wrong emphasis to a key factor at a given stage may hinder the candidate's presentation of self.

The presentation of self is further influenced by the context of the race and the specific situation of the candidate. Specific qualities that the presentation of self seeks to communicate are only instruments to the relationship the candidate is intent upon developing. Social scientists tend to talk about voting behavior in terms of specific variables and formal models.[1] Candidates and producers, by contrast, appear much more concerned with the summary effects of these influences. While much of electoral research focuses on presidential images, the findings may be relevant in other contexts. Goldenberg and Traugott (1984) is the only quantitative work to date that attempts to integrate the theories of campaign actors (managers) with impressions left among voters.

In limiting our view, and in many cases our analyses, to predicting the vote, quantifying the content of ads, or examining the psychological predispositions of the voter, we lose much. This analysis has attempted to step back and take the broadest possible view. In listening to the candidates talk about their strategies, their goals, their analyses of what went right (and wrong), we have gained some perspective on why the political campaign may not be the ideal arena for issue debate. That many voters lack strong issue-orientations has been clear for some time. The role that candidates (and media producers) see for issues in the campaign has been less developed.

Counting the occurrences of issue statements or personal information in ads is a task better suited to accountants than to those who would gain insights into why viewers react as they do. To truly see the ad we must view it as the audience does. Audiences do not generally spend their time dissecting the message. Rather they form impressions based on the mood, which may have been created by background music, the sharpness of the visual images, and the persuasiveness of the verbal content. The specific information in a message that is communicated in thirty to sixty seconds may be less durable than these impressions formed in the viewer's mind.[2] In focusing our attention on viewer recall of campaign information, we may be measuring the wrong thing. We must measure the impressions created, and their duration and change, as well as the intentions of candidates and producers, and the effectiveness of the presentation.

The campaign is a courtship. The candidates must be properly introduced; there is a period of wooing; and an ultimate acceptance or rejection of the suitor. The dilemma of all candidates is one of how to achieve intimate connection with their potential constituency. Perhaps political scientists have been too harsh in their prescriptions that rational voters must exercise judgment on the basis of issue proximity.[3] One could argue that issue proximity is really quite superficial and that it is only useful when the voters have a sense of knowing the candidate "as a man." The revelation of a candidate's character is critical to establishing the intimate connection, and thus to winning political support.

The candidates themselves, not unexpectedly, do not think in terms of standard social science variables. They see essentially two factors operating in the campaign process. There are an information factor and an intimacy factor at work. These "factors" are aptly named because they represent summary influences. The information factor may include, but is not limited to, issue proximity. It can also include basic information about the candidate's birthplace, previous career experience, public service, family life, ideology, and values. It serves primarily to increase familiarity with the candidate, to generate awareness. The information factor can also serve as a mechanism for raising questions about performance in office—or potential performance in office. It can reflect positive and negative information, and may be critical in the acquaintanceship and deterioration stages of the courtship campaign.

The intimacy factor also represents the sum of many influences. The intimacy factor may include, but is not limited to, evaluations of candidates. It reflects voter comfort with the candidate and implies a judgment about the candidate based on the facts presented by the candidate and what they mean. It is the view into the candidate's inner self that feeds expectations about the future. The intimacy factor, like the information factor, may have positive and negative components. It is critical in the building and continuation stages of the courtship campaign.

Videostyle may affect the political process in two ways. First, as candidates turn increasingly to the use of political advertising, the choices voters are making are implicitly not only between two candidates but also between producers. The "style" of the ad is not just a product of the candidate. The research on individual voters has repeatedly confirmed that large segments of the public rely on the easiest and cheapest cognitive mechanisms for making political decisions. To the extent that political ads inform those choices, the race is not just a race between two candidates. It is also a competition of producer philosophies.

Political spots are explicit attempts by the candidates and producers to control the context within which voting choices are made. An issue or candidate quality is talked about, or not talked about, in an effort to raise or dampen its salience. The kind of information presented is influenced by the philosophy of the principal actors in the campaign.

The second way in which videostyle may shape the political process is in developing in the candidate new skills necessary to this kind of effective self-presentation. Different forms of communication sharpen different skills. The extent to which the skills developed in a media campaign spill over and affect later performance in office is a separate but related subject much in need of study.

The interpersonal communication of home style is conducive to transmitting certain types of information more readily than the mass communication of videostyle. The need to anticipate reactions—as opposed to thinking on your feet—may have something to do with what appears to be an emerging obsession by political leaders with opinion tracking. When the congressman communicates personally with his district he gets immediate responses to his presentation of self. When a senator communicates through television with his constituents, responses to his presentation of self can only be detected through monitoring of public opinion.

The control candidates can exert over their presentation of selves through editing of political spots is balanced by the flow of other information about themselves that they cannot control.[4] The press, and their opponents, can be counted upon to introduce less flattering information into the race. Thus, candidates will not be able to go from place to place making contradictory promises because such conflicting statements have a high probability of appearing on the nightly news. For those whose media diet does not include the news, there are the attack spots of the challenger to bring the warts of the incumbent into full view. Similarly, the incumbent's campaign effort will seek to show the flaws of his challenger.

Reading between the lines of Fenno's analysis it is clear that at the core of home style is the candidate's personality. It is the congressman's personality that determines how comfortable he is with a particular "presentation of self." The unique communication characteristics of political advertising place strategy, rather than personality, at the core of videostyle. This is readily apparent in the discussion of candidates and producers alike, all of whom refer to the accomplishment of particular goals in the discussion of their political spots.

The commonalities apparent in these three cases should in no way encourage the view that there is one successful videostyle. In fact, it is the ability to see the unique aspects of each opponent and each race that may yield the greatest political success over time. It is axiomatic that whatever worked last time will not work the next time. The opponent will be prepared to effectively counter whatever was the cause of his/her predecessor's downfall. Nevertheless, some general strategic principles representing plausible hypotheses much in need of systematic examination can be extracted from the preceding chapters. These general principles, the ten commandments of running for the U.S. Senate, if you will, may guide, but should not dictate, campaign strategy.

1. Thou shalt run against someone you can beat. (This is not necessarily your opponent. Run against an unpopular incumbent president, the national parties, the Senate as an institution, thirty years of Democratic rule. . . .)

In Magic State and in Sunstate the incumbent senators ran races against potentially strong challengers. Senator Niceguy chose to run against the Washington bureaucracy and to give his opponent as little recognition as possible. His strategic use of surrogates to answer his challenger further diminished the credibility of his opponent—a subtle indicator to voters that Goodchance was not really worthy of attention. Senator Niceguy preferred to define the race as a challenge to such agencies as the Social Security Administration and Bureau of Land Management. Framing the choice in this context allowed his campaign to profit from widely held negative perceptions of "bureaucracy" generally. Furthermore, he could be certain that neither SSA nor BLM would respond to his charges with a counterattack.

Both Senator Cloistered and Senator Niceguy answered the challenge by running against someone they could beat. Senator Cloistered moved quickly to associate his opponent with the national Democratic party and then ran against the idea of thirty years of Democratic control of the Congress. This was a false issue since Democratic control of the Senate ended in 1980, and his opponent had certainly not served in the Senate in the thirty years prior. It was, nevertheless, effective.

Senator Doright, of Outland, attempted a similar strategy, but with mixed results. He attempted to focus attention on his successful skirmishes with the Washington bureaucracy. His opponent countered with information linking him to that establishment—and implying that he was part of the problem. In general, however, it is clear that candidates who are able to define the context of the choice the voter will make are more successful than those who do not. The unsuccessful challengers focused, or allowed attention to be focused on: a popular U.S. president, a popular incumbent, and/or their own connections to unpopular policies and party organizations.

2. Thou shalt give people a reason to vote for you that is consistent with your strengths as a candidate.

Corollary: 2a. Focus Attention. Focus, focus, focus. (The focus can be personal appeal, issue agreement, identification with the state, whatever your most attractive attribute is—focus.)

Giving people a reason to vote for you that is consistent with your strengths as a candidate may seem obvious, but it is perhaps more difficult than anything else. Candidates appear to be more concerned about issues than producers are, and in most cases candidates exercised final decisions about what would be aired. Ideology and self-perception seem to have an inordinate influence here. The candidate who believes in issue voting has difficulty avoiding issues—even if the constituency he hopes to win disagrees with him on the issues. The hope of converting them dies hard. Similarly, candidates who interpret election results as issue mandates are led to emphasize issue positions. This is in part what led to the slide in support for Senator Doright. His 1976 campaign had stressed his personal character and values, and he interpreted that success as support for specific policies. Thus, he attempted to run for reelection on the basis of issues, neglecting the power of his personal character, which had proved so compelling previously.

The challenger in Sunstate, Thomas Popular, mourns his decision to try to "beguile the voters" with his personality. But the content of the ads he released reveals that they do not, for the most part, allow the viewer/voter to look into his character. His strengths as a candidate are his sense of humor, energy, and personal charm—little of which is communicated. In a conservative state this moderately liberal candidate attempted to discuss policies on which he disagreed with a good many potential constituents, and he further alienated potential support by attacking the revered president.

In Magic State, Matt Niceguy epitomizes success in focusing attention on his strengths as a candidate. The senator looks deeply into the soul of his state—and communicates his vision with empathy, respect, and affection. The whole ad, from background music, to setting, to use of color, to pace, to visual and verbal content, expresses his comment "I am Magic State" without arrogance or conceit. Niceguy acknowledges that painting an issue identity is difficult. He sees that issues do not seem to be guiding, yet he is aware that they can make him vulnerable. Niceguy is able to blend issues information and values in a revealing presentation of himself that reestablishes his close identification with the state and demonstrates once again that he is an attentive suitor.

3. (incumbents only) Thou shalt not directly attack. Let credible surrogates do it for you.

Corollary: 3a. Thou shalt not answer attacks directly either—surrogates should be used here too.

It is in the nature of being challenged that an incumbent senator will be attacked. In the best of all possible worlds such attacks will not be personal, vicious, or slanderous— but they *may* be. It is the view of this author that the attack is less important to the courtship process than the response it elicits. Given a previously solid relationship, the incumbent can generally assume that he will be, to a certain extent, given the benefit of the doubt. Overreacting will make for a suspicious constituency. (What do we really think when confronted with a public statement like "I am not a crook?")

In the case of attack, the focus of attention can be shifted by using credible surrogates to respond to charges. This strategy has a dual purpose. Not only is the impression created that the charge is too ludicrous to merit a direct response, but it allows the incumbent to maintain dignity. A credible surrogate can be another member of the party, another senator or public official, a campaign aide, or other person that can reasonably be assumed (by the public) to know the truth. Raising doubts about the credibility of the attacker achieves two things. First, it discredits the charge, and, second, it diverts the energies of the challenger to defensive rather than offensive play. Successful candidates in this book, without exception, were able to discredit attacks upon their qualifications.

4. (challengers only) Thou shalt always attack, but never personally. The burden of proof is on you. *In contrasting yourself with the incumbent,* raise all appropriate ques-

tions about qualifications, performance, attentiveness to the state.

Corollary: 4a. Thou shalt always answer attacks immediately and directly.

Perhaps obviously, the role of the challenger is to challenge. Thus, there is a public expectation that the challenger will raise questions about the performance (and possibly the character of) the incumbent. Because of this expectation, the challenger must worry less about distancing himself from attacks than about raising sufficient doubt about the incumbent so that he will be given a closer look. (One does not look elsewhere for a new romance when utterly satisfied with the present suitor.)

The challenger in Outland, Johnny Fasttrack is more successful at this than his counterparts in Sunstate and Magic State. Unable to compete with the incumbent, Harold Doright, on the basis of personal integrity, he successfully casts selected votes of the incumbent in a unfavorable light, at the same time voicing his agreement with noncontroversial values in the state. The positive, trailed by negative, airing sequence of his spots is a means of controlling the political climate.

The challenge Robert Goodchance attempted to raise about the record of Matt Niceguy was quite similar. Unfortunately, getting that question across was made more difficult by his own need to explain his past. Prior associations with Ted Kennedy, unpopular in this Republican state, and Goodchance's poor attendance record in the state legislature may have diverted public attention, as well as his own energy, from the challenge.

The difficulties of Thomas Popular's challenge were not unlike those of Goodchance. He too had been associated with Kennedy and unpopular positions of the national Democratic party. His call to the incumbent Senator Daniel Cloistered to defend his record was perhaps more poorly articulated than the efforts of Goodchance and Fasttrack.

5. Thou shalt pay attention to local political norms, especially in media portrayals of image. If an out-of-state producer is used, be especially sensitive to local tastes.

People may be the same the world over, but customs are not. The citizens of most states feel that they are different, "special," and the campaign that recognizes this will be successful. The winning candidates in this book had producers who effectively used visual imagery to reflect the unique political culture of the constituents they were courting. This ability to use local norms in communicating personal attractiveness, similarity, and reciprocity can be a critical element in establishing intimate connection. Part of the intimacy arises from evoking the sensation that the candidate is known. But intimate connection implies that the viewer/voter is *known to the candidate* as well. Is it obvious to note that intimacy works both ways?

Again, the campaign of Matt Niceguy epitomizes the value in paying attention to local tastes. His spots not only reveal the quality of his character and performance, but they also reveal his understanding of the quintessential Magic Stater. Visually, one immediately links the people in his casework spots to a time, a place, and a way of life.

The "hearts and flowers" spots produced for Senator Cloistered act in much the same way. These spots have slightly more emphasis on showing the tender, human side of the senator and slightly less emphasis on showing his vision of the character of the state. Given the differences in the ways Niceguy and Cloistered were perceived going into their respective races, this is probably wise.

Only one of Robert Goodchance's spots captures his character and his vision of the state effectively: the so-called "family" spot. None of the ads released by the Popular campaign reflects this rule. Only one ("frontier spirit") of the 1982 spots released by Doright's campaign illustrate this principle, although all of his 1976 spots did so.

6. Thou shalt be the first to define your image and, if at all possible, your opponent's image too. It is harder to change an impression than to create one.

If there is such a thing as a "challenger's advantage" counterpart to incumbent advantage, this may well be it. The challenger comes into the race with a unique opportunity in the presentation of self. Senator Doright's 1976 move from a career in public service to politics is the purest case illustrating this principle. Hal Doright's campaign introduced him to the state by showing his positive traits and mirroring the incumbent Senator Losttouch's difficulties in terms of those same traits. Hal Doright was shown as the epitome of integrity, while doubts about the incumbent's ethics were evoked. Actually, the incumbent was never directly charged with anything more than having served a long time in office.

Robert Goodchance shared this unique opportunity to paint an identity. He had never run statewide before his challenge to Senator Niceguy. Thus, he could frame the context in which his acquaintanceship with the public would begin. The same was true for Thomas Popular. Johnny Fasttrack, on the other hand, began his challenge with about half the state knowing him, based on his previous statewide campaign and his having held a state office.

Matt Niceguy did a particularly effective job of defining his opponent's image. Robert Goodchance's identity was "painted" as young, ambitious, a lawyer—none of which could be denied. The way that these characteristics were communicated, nevertheless, carried strong negative connotations.

The incumbents in these 1982 races began the campaign as known entities. Their relationships with the public were well established. For them, the courtship analogy may be somewhat strained; and it may be more useful to think in terms of marriage. Creating that initial spark is no longer the problem for these candidates. Instead they must seek to keep the romance alive. Are they so familiar that their constituents have become bored? Have too many areas of dissimilarity arisen over the course of a term of office? Have they taken their supporters for granted and thus allowed the perception of unequal responsibility, commitment, or reward to take root? Have they psychologically left the state behind? These are the seeds of defeat.

For the incumbents, defining an image means re-evoking the positive sentiments that led to victory in the first place. It means reassuring those who have been alienated by any of their decisions while in office that disagreements will exist regardless of whom they elect and that the areas of shared values mean more than the small disagreements. It means increasing the salience of a shared history and calling attention to the desirability of continuing to share the future.

7. Thou shalt avoid carrying the baggage of anyone else (the national parties, an unpopular incumbent president, or other national figure). *Distance can be as important as focus.*

Two of the challengers, Robert Goodchance and Thomas Popular, faced the dilemma of how to drop unpopular associations. Both candidates were associated with locally unpopular issue positions of the national Democratic party on gun control, abortion, the equal rights amendment, and other controversial issues. Neither candidate supported the national party's stance. Such a situation is what is meant by a candidate's "carrying the baggage" of the national party. It is one thing to carry the banner of your own ideological commitments and quite another to be burdened with ideological positions with which you don't agree.

Either incumbents or challengers may be burdened in this way. Harold Doright, in some senses, was victimized by his service in the previous Senate. He was associated with the policies that had produced high unemployment in Outland. His predecessor, Senator Losttouch, carried the baggage of the corrupt Congress in which he served.

How does a candidate drop the baggage, or better yet, hand it back to those who would leave him holding the bag? This is an area where the information factor can be used to advantage. The more aware that voters are of the candidates' true values, the less likely it is that candidates will be burdened with unpopular associations. While the basic facts about a candidate and his issue positions may not do much for establishing "intimate connection" with the voters, increasing constituent awareness levels can do a lot for insulating incumbents and improving challenger credibility. The intimacy factor can also play a role here. When Senator Niceguy was accused of voting himself a pay raise, he was able to draw upon trust—"do you really think I'd do that"—and his opponent's credibility took a nosedive.

8. Thou shalt never tell, always show. Drama is important in getting the voter's attention. Television is a visual medium, use that quality to *show* what you are, what you stand for. The candidate with subtlety gets extra points.

A developing body of experimental research on media effects suggests that the impact of television is at once subtle and complex.[5] When the visual and audio messages conflict, it is the visual to which the receiver attributes the greatest weight.[6] Visual images may be easier to recall than verbal messages. Perhaps most important, a process which Krugman and Hartley term "passive learning" may operate.[7] Passive learning emphasizes what is "caught" rather than "taught" as the driving force in retention of information.

Most of the media producers interviewed for this book have somehow intuited that the visual image may overpower all else. Combined with the production techniques, the visual may provide viewers with subtle cues that potentially render the audio message irrelevant. Neil South, producer for Senator Daniel Cloistered, is most sensitive to the need to take advantage of the visual power of television. His "hearts and flowers" spot reveals a side of the senator that in all likelihood, interpersonal communication would never permit. Whether this makes the spot a "clever ad" that deceives the public or simply a creative solution to the problem of negative public perceptions of a candidate shall be left to the reader to decide. Brad Show, producer for Harold Doright and Matt Niceguy, demonstrates in several spots a talent for the use of latent symbolism in his choice of settings, lightings, and the fortuitous occurrence of rainbows.

This analysis sidesteps the issue of whether the above-mentioned spots actually had the intended effect—other than by citing the results of elections, of candidate polls where available, and by recording candidate and producer perceptions in the absence of other data. The ads are presented to the reader in much the same way that the viewer might experience them. It is crucial to look at the spot as a whole, to look at its presentation within the context of the race, to look at its evocative qualities, and to look at the strategy behind the presentation. What works on the radio will not work on television, because of the unique characteristics of each medium. Radio forces the listener to visualize. Television intrudes into the home of the viewer with its own images. Interpersonal and print communication have still other features rendering them quite different. The successful candidates in these races were sensitive to the characteristics of the communication channel they utilized and its potential effects on the presentation of their messages.

9. Thou shalt keep communications parallel. If a question is raised through one medium, answer it through the same medium to reach the same audience. Answering through a different medium only gives the charge more publicity.

Several of the candidates interviewed talked about the charges that were made against them in the personal appearances of their opponents. In some cases, these charges were answered through the mass media. This is a risky strategy. The risk that is taken is that in answering the charge, the candidate will communicate it to people who did not initially hear it. Thus the negative information is spread.

In using the same channel of communication to respond to an attack, a candidate maximizes the probability that he will reach the same audience his opponent did. In Robert Goodchance's case he asked the newspaper which printed inaccurate things about his campaign for a retraction. Eventually he got it. In Johnny Fasttrack's case, he answered the televised charges of the incumbent through his own television spot, in turn prompting the incumbent's airing of a revised spot.

In some circumstances the ideal response is through a press conference. This is the strategy used by Matt Niceguy in explaining the attacks on his voting record. His reply appeared on the nightly news, giving it greater credibility than if he had simply aired another ad.[8] The press conference format allowed him to reach newspaper readers, television news viewers, and radio listeners simultaneously. His tracking of public opinion had revealed that the charges had been widely received, so he had nothing to lose in making his appeal through multiple mediums. Indeed, he had everything to gain.

10. Thou shalt not underestimate thy challenger. Calculate unique strengths and weaknesses and address your campaign to these.

Every candidate comes to the race with some unique strengths and capabilities. Harold Doright has unshakable, unquestionable integrity. His first campaign for office, and subsequent performance in office, confirmed this aspect of his character. Senator Daniel Cloistered's strength is in his ability to articulate the values he shares with his constituents. Senator Matthew Niceguy brings inordinate understanding of, empathy for, and respect for, his constituents into the race.

The challengers bring different capabilities to their campaigns. Johnny Fasttrack demonstrates an acute sense of political timing and a knack for creating a vulnerability in his opponents where others saw none. Thomas Popular is widely acknowledged to be a formidable challenger based on his charm and personal appeal. Robert Goodchance's unique strengths are his energy and dedication to the campaign. He is a hard worker.

Voters do not always vote for a candidate. Sometimes they vote against them. Thus, it is not just strengths that candidates bring to the race, but also vulnerabilities. Doright's vulnerability is philosophical. His interpretation of voting outcomes focuses so heavily on issues that it does not allow for him to focus sufficiently on the intimate connection he needs with constituents. It is this author's speculation that people were voting against Senator Losttouch in 1976 as much as for Doright. Fasttrack's supporters in 1982 are also voting against the incumbent Doright as much as for Fasttrack. Senator Cloistered's vulnerability is also intimate connection. The senator has an overprotective staff, who unintentionally isolate him from the very people with whom he needs a connection. He is difficult to get to, but he is not as arrogant, cold, or dogmatic as reputation would have it. Some of the negative public perceptions his producer discusses may stem from this very inaccessibility, which is, in part, a staff problem. But the voters will inevitably hold the candidate to account, not his staff (at least not directly). Senator Niceguy's vulnerability lies in his inability to increase voter identifications of him with his policy accomplishments while continuing to reveal his inner self and his understanding of the state.

What about the weaknesses of the challengers? Again, this is a speculative assessment. Johnny Fasttrack's weakness is his own perception that communicating his inner self amounts to nothing more than "trying to be a nicer guy." Character counts, and voters care about it. Without the revelation of character, there is no opportunity for emotional connection with the state to be established. His political future holds plenty of opportunity for strategic missteps. Thomas Popular's weakness is the flipside of Fasttrack's. He emphasized intimacy strategically but not in the execution of his ads. His attempts to build an issue-information bond with constituents failed in large part because of the local context in which he raised the issues. Robert Goodchance's vulnerability as a candidate stems from a lack of resources. His campaign suffered from too little awareness among the public, too little money to buy exposure, and too many links to the national Democratic party in a Republican-leaning state.

This study has traded scope for depth. The rich detail gleaned from these three cases can be used to generate hypotheses to be investigated more systematically later. It is difficult and expensive to attempt to bring together in one study extensive analysis of voters' attitudes and exposure to campaign materials, theories held by candidates and other campaign actors, and content analysis of political spots and news coverage of the campaign. Nevertheless, it is hoped that this work will stimulate others to view campaigns as a courtship, and that the courtship perspective will encourage researchers to look at the relationships between and among all actors in the campaign, the process of relationship building, and the impact of the political environment and context on those relationships.

Notes

Chapter One

1. Erving Goffman, *The Presentation of Self in Everyday Life*, (New York: Doubleday, 1959), and Richard F. Fenno, Jr., *Home Style: House Members in Their Districts* (Boston: Little, Brown, 1978).

2. However, some of this research is cited in the pages that follow. For examples of the research on media effects, see Dreyer, "Media Use and Electoral Choices: Some Political Consequences of Information Exposure," *Public Opinion Quarterly* 35, no.4 (1971): 544–53; Goldenberg and Traugott, "Mass Media Effects on Recognizing and Rating Candidates in U.S. Senate Elections," paper presented at the Dwight P. Griswold–E.C. Ames Conference on Mass Media and Congressional Elections (1986); and Tichnor, Donohue, and Olien "Mass Media Flow and Differential Growth in Political Knowledge," *Public Opinion Quarterly* 34, no. 2 (1970): 159–70.

3. Patterson looks at the proportion of campaign budgets devoted to media expenses in "Money Rather Than TV Ads Judged 'Root Cause' of Election Costliness," *Television/Radio Age* 44 (1983): 130–32.

4. Michael Robinson, "Television and American Politics," *The Public Interest* 48 (1977): 1–40.

5. Portions of this interview were previously published in Kaid and Davidson, "Elements of Videostyle: Candidate Presentation Through Television Advertising" in *New Perspectives on Political Advertising*, ed. Kaid, Nimmo, and Sanders (Carbondale: Southern Illinois Univ. Press, 1986), 184–209.

6. Roper Organization, *Trends in Attitudes toward Television and Other Media: A Twenty-Four-Year Review* (New York: Television Information Office, 1983).

7. Herbert E. Krugman and Eugene L. Hartley, "Passive Learning from Television," *Public Opinion Quarterly* 34, no. 2, (1970):184.

8. Doris A. Graber, "Personal Qualities in Presidential Images: The Contribution of the Press," *Midwest Journal of Political Science* 16, no. 1 (1972):42–76; Doris A. Graber, "Press and TV as Opinion Resources in Presidential Campaigns," *Public Opinion Quarterly* 40, no. 3 (1976):285–304; Richard A. Joslyn, "The Content of Political Spot Ads," *Journalism Quarterly* 57 (1980):92–98.

9. Theodore White, *The Making of the President 1960* (New York: Pocket Books, 1961).

10. Larry Sabato, *The Rise of Political Consultants* (New York: Basic Books, 1981); Paul Stevens, *I Can Sell You Anything* (New York: Ballantine Books 1972).

11. Gary C. Jacobson, "The Effects of Campaign Spending in Congressional Elections," *American Political Science Review* 72, no. 2 (1978):469–91.

12. John Kingdon, *Candidates for Office: Beliefs and Strategies* (New York: Random House, 1966), is an exception.

13. Charles Wright provides much of the basis for the distinctions drawn here. See *Mass Communication: A Sociological Perspective*, 2nd ed. (New York: Random House, 1975), 5–8.

14. Michael J. Robinson describes the news audience as "inadvertant." See Robinson, "American Political Legitimacy in an Era of Electronic Journalism: Reflections on the Evening News" *Television as a Cultural Force: New Approaches to TV Criticism*, ed. D. Cater and R. Adler (New York: Praeger, 1975).

15. Kingdon (1966) observes the importance of the relationship between style and process in arguing that, "politicians' theories of voting behavior may be related to the whole *style* of politics found in different political systems," p. 39. (Emphasis added.)

16. David Vogler, *The Politics of Congress* (Neston, Mass.: Allyn and Bacon, 1981).

Chapter Two

1. L. Sandy Maisel also makes this point in his book *From Obscurity to Oblivion: Running in the Congressional Primary* (Univ. of Tennessee Press, 1982), 10–11.

2. Abramson, Aldrich, and Rhode examine the role of expectations early in presidential campaigns in *Change and Continuity in the 1980 Election* (Washington, D.C.: Congressional Quarterly Press, 1981).

3. George Levinger, "Toward the Analysis of Close Relationships," *Journal of Experimental Social Psychology* 16, no. 6 (1980): 510–44.

4. Kent Tedin and Richard Murray, "Public Awareness of Congressional Representatives: Recall versus Recognition," *American Politics Quarterly* 7, no. 4 (1979):509–17.

5. Byrne and Murnen describe these threats to the marital relationship as well as one more—physical separation. Physical separation is not considered a serious threat to the political relationship since there is no expectation of the participants' living together. However, psychological distance is a very real threat and is discussed in some detail later. See "Maintaining Loving Relationships," in *The Anatomy of Love*, ed. R. J. Sternberg and M. L. Barnes (New Haven: Yale Univ. Press, 1987).

6. Kaid and Davidson (1986) present a cursory exploration of what videostyle might be. The definition of videostyle used in this book goes beyond the 1986 work in that ad content is not used to define the components of videostyle. Rather, the components are the information and intimacy factors *expressed through* ad content.

7. Goffman, *Presentation of Self*, 9.

8. This argument was presented in Kaid and Davidson, 189.

9. Doris A. Graber, *Processing the News: How People Tame the Information Tide* (New York: Longman, 1984), demonstrates that people process new information by relying on "schemas"—or frames of reference, based on old information which the new information evokes.

10. Charles Atkin and Gary Heald, "Effects of Political Advertising," *Public Opinion Quarterly* 40, no. 2 (1976):216–28.

11. Donald Stokes and Warren Miller, "Party Government and the Salience of Congress," *Public Opinion Quarterly* 26, no. 4 (1962):541.

12. Jacobson, "The Impact of Broadcast Campaigning on Electoral Outcomes," *Journal of Politics* 37, no. 3 (1975):769–93.

13. Richard E. Neustadt's discussion of presidential power characterized presidential influence as teaching in a way similar to that discussed here. See *Presidential Power: The Politics of Leadership From FDR to Carter* (New York: Wiley, 1980), 74.

14. Fenno's (1978) analysis stressed the candidate's development of a style with which he was *personally* comfortable. In the case of television advertising, the candidate's presentation of self may be altered, without necessarily causing him great discomfort, through editing. A media campaign which presents a style too different from the candidate's interpersonal style, however, runs the risk of "boomeranging" as press coverage and personal appearances show voters a different candidate from the one portrayed through the ads.

15. J. W. Kingdon (1966) looks at the effect of electoral outcomes on candidate perceptions, reaching the same conclusion based on many more cases. However, Goldenberg and Traugott (1984) take issue with this general conclusion based on different study designs and methods, as do Kim and Racheter, "Candidates' Perceptions of Voter Competence: A Comparison of Winning and Losing Candidates," *American Political Science Review* 67, no. 3 (1973):906–93. The cases presented here, using methods similar to Kingdon's, tend to confirm his findings.

Chapter Three

1. See Paul Allen Beck, "Context, Choice, and Consequence: Beaten and Unbeaten Paths Toward a Science of Electoral Behavior," in *Political Science: The Science of Politics*, ed. Herbert Weisberg (New York: Agathon Press, 1986), 241–83.

2. Herbert Weisberg, "Comments on Beck's APSA Theme Paper,"

explores in detail the consequences for the field, of choices not taken (personal communication from Herb Weisberg, Sept. 1983).

3. See for example John Carey, "How Media Shapes Campaigns," *Journal of Communication* 26, no. 2 (1976):50–64; and Jarol B. Manheim, "Can Democracy Survive Television," *Journal of Communication* 76, no. 2 (1976):84–90.

4. See Peter Rossi, "Four Landmarks in Voting Research," in *American Voting Behavior*, ed. Burdick and Brodbeck (New York: Free Press, 1959), 5–54.

5. L. Sandy Maisel (1982) and Edie Goldenberg and Michael Traugott (1984) illustrate very well that incumbents and challengers run very different races—largely because they face such different circumstances and possess such different resources. These studies are representative of more recent work attempting to assess the impact of new campaign techniques on the electoral process.

6. Gary Jacobson and Samuel Kernell, *Strategy and Choice in Congressional Elections* (New Haven: Yale Univ. Press, 1983); Robert Bernstein, "Divisive Primaries Do Hurt: U.S. Senate Races, 1956–1972) *American Political Science Review* 71, no. 2 (June 1977):540–45. The literature on senate elections is sparse, but growing. The reader is referred to Hibbing and Brandes (1983) on the impact of state characteristics on outcomes. Hinkley (1980) and Jacobson (1981) have written about the role of the challenger. Kostroski (1973, 1978) and Tuckel (1983) on the impact of incumbency and Westlye (1983) on competitiveness of the race provide insights into the determinants of outcomes. The reader is referred to Mann and Ornstein (1983) for a broad discussion of the 1982 races and to Goldenberg and Traugott (1986) on the role of the media in candidate recognition and evaluation. Abramowitz (1987) provides the most current quantitative study of Senate races looking at all aspects of the campaign and their effects on outcomes.

7. See Edie N. Goldenberg, Michael W. Traugott, and Frank R. Baumgartner, "Preemptive and Reactive Spending in U.S. House Races," *Political Behavior* 8, no. 1 (1986):3–19.

8. Festinger, Schacter, and Back, 1950; Caplow and Forman, 1950; Nahemow and Lawton, 1975; Ebbeson, Kjos, and Konecni, 1976; Moreland and Zajonc, 1982.

9. Beck, Ward-Hull, and McLear, 1976; Horvath, 1979; Lavrakas,

1975; Gillis and Avis, 1980; Graziano, Brothen, and Berscheid, 1978.

10. Kleinke and Staneski, 1980; Wiggins, Wiggins, and Conger, 1968.

11. Brigham, 1980; and Gillen, 1981.

12. Palmer and Bryne, 1970; Riskind and Wilson, 1982; McAllister and Bregman, 1983.

13. Rosenberg, Bohan, McCafferty, and Harris, 1986.

14. Jellison and Oliver, 1983; Bryne and Nelson, 1965; Neimeyer and Neimeyer, 1981; and Campbell, 1986.

15. See White, "Physical Attractiveness and Courtship Progress," *Journal of Personality and Social Psychology* 39, no. 3 (1980): 660—68.

16. Bryne and Nelson, 1965.

17. Gold, Ryckman, and Mosley, 1984; Hays, 1984.

18. Excerpts from this interview were previously published in Kaid and Davidson (1986).

19. The differences between challenger and incumbent in the advantages each possesses entering the race parallel the differences between companionate and passionate love described by Clyde Hendrick and Susan Hendrick, "A Theory and Method of Love," *Journal of Personality and Social Psychology* 50, no. 2 (1986): 322—402, and by Steck et al, "Care, Need, and Conceptions of Love," *Journal of Personality and Social Psychology* 43, no. 3 (1982):481—91.

20. Morris P. Fiorina, *Retrospective Voting in American National Elections* (New Haven: Yale Univ. Press, 1981), on retrospective evaluations can be reconciled with the future orientation of the candidates and producers interviewed here if one looks at how each is measured. Retrospective evaluations tend to be measured as personality ratings and future promises as issue positions. But future expectations can arise from personality characteristics, just as retrospective evaluations can influence issue position perceptions.

21. Dorothy K. Davidson, "Candidate Evaluations: Rational Instrument or Affective Response?" (Ph.D. diss., Florida State University, 1982), argues that issues may not be useful cues for voting because 1) not all issues arising during a term of office can be anticipated in a campaign, 2) office holders have access to greater

expertise and classified information which could change their positions on issues, and 3) if the candidate cannot be relied on to keep his promises (integrity), issue proximity is of little value.

22. Excerpts from this interview were previously published in Kaid and Davidson (1986).

23. T. Patterson also makes this point in *The Mass Media Election: How Americans Choose Their President* (New York: Praeger, 1980), 135.

24. The "accomplishments" spot produced for Hal Doright in 1982 showed him seated at the front edge of a desk while graphic bullets appeared on the screen describing his activities. In Doright's spot the pictures did not "tell a story." The ad is visually uninteresting, and the audio content is so densely packed with specific information that it is difficult to remember any of it.

25. See Dan Nimmo, *The Political Persuaders: The Techniques of Modern Election Campaigns* (Englewood Cliffs, N.J.: Prentice-Hall, 1970), 26–29, for a discussion of political symbolism in campaigns.

26. Byrne and Murnen (1987).

27. Rusbult, Johnson, and Morrow, "Impact of Couple Patterns of Problem Solving on Distress and Nondistress in Dating Relationships," *Journal of Personality and Social Psychology* 50, no. 3 (1986):744–53, describe these behaviors in relation to the marital situation. Exit and voice are considered constructive behaviors; loyalty and neglect, destructive.

28. Popkin, Gorman, Phillips, and Smith, 1976.

29. See G. Garramone, "Issue versus Image Orientations and Effects of Political Advertising," *Communication Research* 10 (1983):59–76.

Chapter Four

1. This suggests that candidates are less willing to relinquish control over their audio messages than over other aspects of their videostyle.

2. Senator Losttouch's behavior most closely resembles "neglect." Faced with a deteriorating relationship with his constitu-

ents, the senator was unable or unwilling to pull himself away from Washington to rebuild his constituency connection. Subsequent to his defeat, the senator moved to Washington—perhaps indicative of his affinity for D.C. and alienation from his homestate.

3. Rosenfeld and Civikly, *With Words Unspoken* (New York: Holt, Rinehart, Winston, 1976), provide extensive discussion of the meaning attributed to nonverbal cues. See also Kaid and Davidson (1986).

4. *Congressional Quarterly* predicted Doright to be a safe incumbent as late as August 1982.

5. In the year preceding the election, the incumbent's Conservative Coalition support score was in the high eighties (of over a hundred votes). His party unity score was in the mid-eighties; voting participation was in the low nineties. The conservativeness of his record probably fairly accurately represents the moderate-to-conservative nature of the state.

6. Economic indicators for the nation show the jobless rate at 10.1 percent as of September 1982—the highest jobless rate since 1940. In Outland, unemployment exceeded the national rate. The Consumer Price Index for the nation indicated that inflation had been cut in half since Reagan took office, running at 5.9 percent. The prime lending rate had dropped to 12 percent.

7. Kingdon (1966) suggests that winners are more likely to see election outcomes as mandates, regardless of their campaign. In this race, both winner and loser focused on issue implications of the outcome, perhaps an indicator of their deep philosophical commitment to issue politics.

8. Excerpts from this interview were previously published in Kaid and Davidson (1986).

9. Excerpts from this interview were previously published in Kaid and Davidson (1986).

10. Wolfinger and Rosenstone, *Who Votes?* (New Haven: Yale Univ. Press, 1980), paint a demographic portrait of voters.

11. The impact of party identification on the vote was established very early in works such as Campbell, Gurin and Miller, *The Voter Decides* (Chicago: Univ. of Chicago Press, 1954); Lazersfeld, Berelson, and Gaudet, *The People's Choice* (New York: Columbia Univ. Press, 1948); Berelson, Lazersfeld, and McPhee, *Voting* (Chi-

cago: Univ. of Chicago Press, 1954); and Campbell, Converse, Miller, and Stokes, *The American Voter* (New York: Wiley, 1960).

12. This outlook is consistent with the minimalist interpretation of mass media and campaign effects.

13. A considerable amount of attention has been devoted to studying the role of issues in electoral politics. The way that citizens process issue information has been described by Graber (1984, 1976, 1972). The influence of issues in voter behavior can be traced in Campbell, Converse, Miller and Stokes (1960), Kessel (1972), Nie, Verba, and Petrocik (1976), Miller, Miller, Raine, and Brown (1976), Pomper (1972), RePass (1971) and a host of other issue voting studies.

Chapter Five

1. "Largest Turnover in Senate Since 1958" *Congressional Quarterly Weekly Report* (Nov. 6, 1976):3127-29.

2. "Will Money Preserve GOP Gains of 1980?" *Congressional Quarterly Weekly Report* (April 10, 1982):814-16.

3. Excerpts from this interview were previously published in Kaid and Davidson (1986).

4. T.R. Donohue, in "Viewer Perceptions of Color and Black-and-White Paid Political Advertising," *Journalism Quarterly* 50, no. 4 (1973):660, demonstrates that color affects females more positively than males, but increases positive judgments of overall quality of commercials for both sexes. In this spot, the use of black and white is for symbolic dramatic effect.

5. T.E. Mann and N.J. Ornstein, *The American Elections of 1982*, (Washington, D.C.: American Enterprise Institute, 1983).

6. Excerpts from this interview were previously published in Kaid and Davidson (1986).

7. G.C. Jacobson, "The Impact of Broadcast Campaigning on Electoral Outcomes," *Journal of Politics* 37, no. 3 (1975):769-93.

Chapter Six

1. See, for example, Kinder, Peters, Abelson, and Fiske (1980); Miller, Wattenberg, and Malanchuk (1986); Conover (1981); and Davidson (1982).

2. Barnett, Serota, and Taylor, "Campaign Communication and Attitude Change," *Human Communication Research* 2, no. 3 (1976): 327–44, find that four factors are causally related to attitude change—the number of new messages, the number of messages comprising the initial balance point, the amount of discrepancy between old attitudes and the mean position advocated by new messages, and the credibility or significance of the source and/or the salience of the information.

3. This view of rationality has been challenged by Fiorina (1981) and others who have defended the utility of voters' concern with personality and cumulative performance assessments.

4. Barbara Hinkley, "House Reelections and Senate Defeats: The Role of the Challenger," *British Journal of Political Science* 10, no. 4 (1980):441–60, shows that Senate voters exhibit more information and more media contact (especially television contact) than House voters.

5. See Shanto Iyengar, Mark D. Peters, and Donald R. Kinder, "Experimental Demonstrations of the 'Not-So-Minimal' Consequences of Television News Programs," *American Political Science Review* 76, no. 4 (1982):848–58; also Goldenberg and Traugott (1984).

6. Gina Garramone, "Issue Versus Image Orientation and Effects of Political Advertising," *Communication Research* 10 (1983): 59–76.

7. Krugman and Hartley, "Passive Learning from Television," *Public Opinion Quarterly* 34, no. 2 (1970):184–90.

8. See Virginia Andreoli and Stephen Worchel, "Effects of Media Communicator and Message Position on Attitude Change," *Public Opinion Quarterly* 42, no. 1 (1978):59–70.

Bibliography

Abramowitz, Alan. "Explaining Senate Election Outcomes." Paper presented at the American Political Science Association meetings, Chicago, Ill., 1987.

Abramson, Paul; Aldrich, John H.; and Rhode, David W. *Change and Continuity in the 1980 Elections*. Rev. ed. Washington, D.C.: Congressional Quarterly Press, 1983.

Andreoli, Virginia, and Worchel, Stephen. "Effects of Media Communicator and Message Position on Attitude Change." *Public Opinion Quarterly* 42, no. 1 (1978):59–70.

Arterton, Christopher F. *Media Politics*. Lexington, Mass.: Lexington Books, 1984.

Atkin, Charles E., and Heald, Gary E. "Effects of Political Advertising." *Public Opinion Quarterly* 40, no. 2 (1976):216–228.

Barnett, George A.; Serota, Kim B.; and Taylor, James A. "Campaign Communication and Attitude Change." *Human Communication Research* 2, no. 3 (1976):327–44.

Battlin, Tom C. "Directing." In *Television Broadcasting*, ed. R. L. Hilliard, 211–66. New York: Hastings House, 1978.

Beck, Paul Allen. "Choice, Context, and Consequence: Beaten and Unbeaten Paths toward a Science of Electoral Behavior." In *Political Science: The Science of Politics*, ed. H. Weisberg, 241–83. New York: Agathon Press, 1986.

Beck, Sally Bell; Ward-Hull, Christine I.; and McLear, Paul M. "Variables Related to Women's Somatic Preferences of the Male and Female Body." *Journal of Personality and Social Psychology* 34, no. 6 (1976):1200–20.

Berelson, Bernard R.; Lazersfeld, Paul F.; and McPhee, William N. *Voting*. Chicago: Univ. of Chicago Press, 1954.

Bernstein, Robert A. "Divisive Primaries Do Hurt: U.S. Senate Races, 1956–1972." *American Political Science Review* 71, no. 2 (June 1977):540–45.

Brigham, John C. Limiting Conditions of the "Physical Attractiveness Stereotype: Attributions about Divorce." *Journal of Research and Personality* 14 (1980):365–75.

Bryne, Donn, and Murnen, S. "Maintaining Loving Relationships." In *The Anatomy of Love*, ed. R.J. Sternberg and M.L. Barnes. New Haven: Yale Univ. Press, 1987.

Bryne, Donn, and Nelson, Don. "Attraction as a Linear Function of Proportion of Positive Reinforcements." *Journal of Personality and Social Psychology*, 1, no. 6 (1965):659–63.

Campbell, Angus; Converse, Phillip E.; Miller, Warren E.; and Stokes, Donald E. *The American Voter*. New York: Wiley, 1960.

Campbell, Angus; Gurin, Gerald; and Miller, Warren E. *The Voter Decides*. Chicago: Univ. of Chicago Press, 1954.

Campbell, Jennifer D. "Similarity and Uniqueness: The Effects of Attribute Type, Relevance, and Individual Differences in Self-Esteem and Depression. *Journal of Personality and Social Psychology* 50, no. 2 (1986):281–94.

Caplow, F., and Forman, R. Neighborhood Interaction in a Homogeneous Community." *American Sociological Review* 15 (1950): 357–66.

Carey, John. "How Media Shape Campaigns." *Journal of Communication* 26, no. 2 (1976):50–64.

Congressional Quarterly Weekly Reports:

Oct. 9, 1976. "Congressional Races: No Signs of Upheaval," 2769–2869.

Oct. 23, 1976. "New Right Plans Move to Change Congress," 3027–31.

Oct. 23, 1976. "New Federal Election Law Has Its Critics," 3032–37.

Oct. 30, 1976. "Signs Point to a Congress like the Last One," 3072–73.

Nov. 6, 1976. "Largest Turnover in Senate Since 1958," 3127–29.

Feb. 13, 1982. "Senators' Fundraising: Millions for Self-Defense," 278–79.

Feb. 27, 1982. "Money Flows to the Right in 1982 Campaign," 482.

April 10, 1982. "Will Money Pressure GOP Gains of 1980," 814–16.

May 1, 1982. "PAC Politics: The Power of Information," 1027.

Aug. 14, 1982. "Senate Campaign Strategies: The Early Money Approach," 1987–88.

Sept. 4, 1982. "In the Senate of the Eighties Team Spirit Has Given Way to the Rule of Individuals," 2175–82.

Sept. 11, 1982. "Searching for the Sleeper Senate Election," 2287.

Oct. 16, 1982. "The Campaign Finance System No One Asked for," 2703.

Oct. 16, 1982. "Well-Funded Safe Incumbents Use Money in Diverse Ways," 2691–92.

Oct. 16, 1982. Tactical Errors, Disunity, Blunt New Right Social Legislation," 2675–78.

Oct. 23, 1982. "Direct-Mail Bids Do Not Ensure Pot of Gold," 2714–15.

———. "Elections '82: Referendum on Reagonomics?" 2716–19.

Oct. 23, 1982. "Reagan, the Economy, and the Polls," 2719.

Oct. 30, 1982. "Senate Bids Emerge as Finale to House-Dominated Season," 2747.

Oct. 30, 1982. "The 1982 Turnout Question: Voters Angry or Depressed?" 2748–51.

Nov. 6, 1982, "Senate Election: A Dull Affair Compared to 1980's Upheaval," 2789–94.

Conover, Pamela Johnston. "Political Cues and the Perception of Candidates." *American Politics Quarterly* 9 (1981):427–48.

Davidson, Dorothy K. "Candidate Evaluations: Rational Instrument of Affective Response?" Ph.D. diss., Florida State University, 1982.

Dexter, Lewis A. *Elite and Specialized Interviewing*. Evanston, Ill.: Northwestern Univ., 1970.

Diamond, Edwin, and Bates, Stephen. *The Spot*. Cambridge, Mass.: MIT Press, 1984.

Donohue, Thomas R. "Viewer Perceptions of Color and Black-and-White Paid Political Advertising." *Journalism Quarterly* 50, no. 4 (1973):660–70.

Dreyer, Edward C. "Media Use and Electoral Choices: Some Political Consequences of Information Exposure." *Public Opinion Quarterly* 35, no. 4 (1971–72):544–53.

Ebbesen, Ebbe B.; Kjos, Glenn L.; and Konecni, Vladimir J. "Spatial Ecology: Its Effects on the Choice of Friends and Enemies." *Journal of Experimental Social Psychology* 12, no. 6 (1976): 505–18.

Fenno, Richard F., Jr. *Home Style: House Members in Their Districts*. Boston: Little Brown, 1978.

Festinger, Leon; Schachter, Stanley; and Back, Kurt. *Social Pressures in Informal Groups: A Study of a Housing Community*. New York: Harper, 1950.

Fiorina, Morris P. *Retrospective Voting in American National Elections*. New Haven: Yale Univ. Press, 1981.

Garramone, Gina. "Issue versus Image Orientation and Effects of Political Advertising. *Communication Research* 10 (1983): 59–76.

Gillen, Barry. "Physical Attractiveness: A Determinant of Two Types of Goodness. *Personality and Social Psychology Bulletin* 7, no. 2 (1981):277–81.

Gillis, John Stuart, and Avis, Walter E. "The Male-Taller Norm in Mate Selection. *Personality and Social Psychology Bulletin* 6, no. 3 (1980):396–401.

Goffman, Erving. *The Presentation of Self in Everyday Life*. New York: Doubleday, 1959.

Gold, Joel A.; Ryckman, Richard M.; and Mosley, Norman R. "Romantic Mood Induction and Attraction to a Dissimilar Other: Is Love Blind?" *Personality and Social Psychology Bulletin* 10, no. 3 (1984):358–68.

Goldenberg, Edie, and Traugott, Michael. *Campaigning for Congress*. Washington, D.C.: Congressional Quarterly Press, 1984.

———. "Mass Media Effects on Recognizing and Rating Candidates in U.S. Senate Elections." Paper presented at the Dwight P. Griswold–E.C. Ames Conference on Mass Media and Congressional Elections, Nebraska Wesleyan University, Lincoln, Nebr., 1986.

Goldenberg, Edie; Traugott, Michael; and Baumgartner, Frank R. "Preemptive and Reactive Spending in U.S. House Races." *Political Behavior* 8, no. 1 (1986):3–19.

Graber, Doris A. "Personal Qualities in Presidential Images: The Contribution of the Press." *Midwest Journal of Political Science* 16, no. 1 (1972):46–76.

———. "Press and TV as Opinion Resources in Presidential Campaigns." *Public Opinion Quarterly* 40, no. 3 (1976):285–303.

———. *Mass Media and American Politics*. Washington, D.C.: Congressional Quarterly Press, 1980.

———. *Processing the News: How People Tame the Information Tide*. New York: Longman, 1984.

Graziano, William; Brothen, Thomas; and Berscheid, Ellen. "Height and Attraction: Do Men and Women See Eye to Eye?" *Journal of Personality* 46, no. 1 (1978):128–48.

Hays, R.B. "The Development and Maintenance of Friendships." *Journal of Social and Personal Relations* 1 (1984):75–98.

Hendrick, Clyde, and Hendrick, Susan. "A Theory and Method of Love." *Journal of Personality and Social Psychology* 50, no. 2 (1986):392–402.

Hershey, Marjorie R. *The Making of Campaign Strategy*. Lexington, Mass.: Heath, 1974.

Hibbing, John R., and Brandes, Sara L. "State Population and the Electoral Process." *American Journal of Political Science* 27, no. 4 (1983):808–19.

Hinkley, Barbara. "House Reelections and Senate Defeats: The Role of the Challenger." *British Journal of Political Science*, 10, no. 4 (Oct. 1980):441–60.

Horvath, Theodore. "Correlates of Physical Beauty in Men and Women." *Social Behavior and Personality* 7, no. 2 (1979): 145–51.

Iyengar, Shanto; Peters, Mark D.; and Kinder, Donald R. "Experimental Demonstrations of the 'Not-So-Minimal' "Consequences of Television News Programs." *American Political Science Review* 76, no. 4 (1982): 848–58.

Jacobson, Gary C. "The Impact of Broadcast Campaigning on Electoral Outcomes." *Journal of Politics* 37, no. 3 (1975): 769–93.

———. "The Effects of Campaign Spending in Congressional Elections." *American Political Science Review* 72, no. 2 (1978): 469–91.

———. "Congressional Elections, 1978: The Case of the Vanishing Challengers." In *Congressional Elections*, ed. L.S. Maisel and J. Cooper, 219–48. Beverly Hills: Sage, 1978.

Jacobson, Gary C., and Kernell, Samuel. *Strategy and Choice in Congressional Elections.* 2nd ed. New Haven: Yale Univ. Press, 1983.

Jamieson, Kathleen Hall, and Campbell, Karlyn Kohrs. *The Interplay of Influence.* Belmont, Calif. Wadsworth, 1983.

Jellison, Jerald M., and Oliver, Deborah F. "Attitude Similarity and Attraction: An Impression Management Approach." *Personality and Social Psychology Bulletin* 9, no. 1 (1983): 111–15.

Joslyn, Richard A. "The Content of Political Spot Ads." *Journalism Quarterly* 57 (1980): 92–98.

Kaid, Lynda L., and Davidson, Dorothy K. "Elements of Videostyle: Candidate Presentation through Television Advertising." In *New Perspectives on Political Advertising*, ed. L.L. Kaid, D. Nimmo, and K. R. Sanders, 184–209. Carbondale: Southern Illinois Univ. Press, 1986.

Kessel, John. "Comment: The Issues in Issue Voting." *American Political Science Review* 66, no. 2 (1982): 459–65.

Kim, Chong Lim, and Racheter, Donald P. "Candidates' Perceptions of Voter Competence: A Comparison of Winning and Losing Candidates." *American Political Science Review*, 67, no. 3 (1973): 906–13.

Kinder, Donald R.; Peters, Mark D.; Abelson, Robert P.; and Fiske, Susan T. "Presidential Prototypes." *Political Behavior*, 2, no. 4 (1980): 315–37.

Kingdon, John W. *Candidates for Office: Beliefs and Strategies.* New York: Random House, 1966.

Kleinke, Chris, and Staneski, Richard A. "First Impressions of Female Bust Size." *Journal of Social Psychology* 110 (1980): 123–34.

Kostroski, Warren Lee. "Party and Incumbency in Post War Senate Elections: Trends, Patterns, and Models." *American Political Science Review* 67, no. 4 (1973): 1213–34.

———. "The Effect of Number of Terms on the Reelection of Senators, 1920–1970." *Journal of Politics* 40, no. 2 (1978): 488–97.

Krugman, Herbert E., and Hartley, Eugene L. Passive learning from Television." *Public Opinion Quarterly* 34, no. 2 (1970): 184–90.

Lavrakas, Paul J. "Female Preferences for Male Physiques." *Journal of Research in Personality* 9, no. 4 (1975): 324–34.

Lazersfeld, Paul F.; Berelson, Bernard R.; and Gaudet, Hazel. *The People's Choice.* 2nd ed. New York: Columbia Univ. Press, 1948.

Levinger, George. "Toward the Analysis of Close Relationships." *Journal of Experimental Social Psychology* 16, no. 6 (1980): 510–44.

Maisel, L. Sandy. *From Obscurity to Oblivion: Running in the Congressional Primary.* Knoxville: Univ. of Tennessee Press, 1982.

Manheim, Jarol B. "Can Democracy Survive Television." *Journal of Communication* 26, no. 2 (1976): 84–90.

Mann, Thomas E. *Unsafe at Any Margin: Interpreting Congressional Elections.* Washington, D.C.: American Enterprise Institute, 1978.

Mann, Thomas E., and Ornstein, Norman J. *The American Elections of 1982.* Washington, D.C.: American Enterprise Institute, 1983.

May, James L., and Hamilton, Phyllis Ann. "Effects of Musically Evoked Affect on Women's Interpersonal Attraction and Perceptual Judgments of Physical Attractiveness of Men." *Motivation and Emotion* 4, no. 3 (1980): 217–28.

McAllister, Hunter A., and Bregman, Norman J. "Self-Disclosure and Liking: An Integration Theory Approach." *Journal of Personality* 51, no. 2 (1983): 202–12.

Meadow, Robert G., and Sigelman, Lee. "Some Effects and Non-effects of Campaign Commercials." *Political Behavior* 4 (1982): 163–75.

Miller, Arthur H.; Miller, Warren E.; Raine, Alden S.; and Brown, Thad A. "A Majority Party in Disarray: Policy Polarization in the

1972 Election." *American Political Science Review* 70, no. 3 (1976):753–78.

Miller, Arthur H.; Wattenberg, Martin P.; and Malanchuk, Oksana. "Schematic Assessments of Presidential Candidates." *American Political Science Review* 80, no. 2 (1986):521–40.

Moreland, Richard L., and Zajonc, Robert B. "Exposure Effects in Person Perceptions: Familiarity, Similarity, and Attraction." *Journal of Experimental Social Psychology* 18, no. 5 (1982): 395–415.

Nahemow, Lucille, and Lawton, M. Powell. "Similarity and Propinquity in Friendship Formation." *Journal of Personality and Social Psychology* 32, no. 2 (1975):205–13.

Neimeyer, Greg J., and Neimeyer, Robert A. "Functional Similarity and Interpersonal Attraction." *Journal of Research in Personality*, 15, no. 4 (1981):427–35.

Neustadt, Richard E. *Presidential Power: The Politics of Leadership From FDR to Carter.* New York: Wiley, 1980.

Nie, Norman H.; Verba, Sidney; and Petrocik, John R. *The Changing American Voter.* Cambridge, Mass.: Harvard Univ. Press, 1976.

Nimmo, Dan. *The Political Persuaders: The Techniques of Modern Election Campaigns.* Englewood Cliffs, N.J.: Prentice-Hall, 1970.
———. "Elections as Ritual Drama." *Society,* 38 (1985):31–38.

Paletz, David L. "The Neglected Context of Congressional Campaigns." *Polity* 4, no. 2 (1971):195–217.

Palmer, John, and Bryne, Donn. "Attraction toward Dominant and Submissive Strangers: Similarity Versus Complementarity." *Journal of Experimental Research in Personality* 4, no. 2 (1970): 108–15.

Patterson, Thomas E. *The Mass Media Election: How Americans Choose Their President.* New York: Praeger, 1980.
———. "Money Rather than TV Ads Judged 'Root Cause' of Election Costliness." *Television/Radio Age,* 44 (1983):130–32.

Permut, Steven E. *Political Marketing: An Approach to Campaign Strategy.* New York: Praeger, 1983.

Pomper, Gerald M. "From Confusion to Clarity: Issues and American Voters 1956–1968." *American Political Science Review* 66, no. 2 (1972):415–28.

Popkin, Samuel; Gorman, John W.; Phillips, Charles; and Smith, Jeffrey A. "Comment: What Have You Done for Me Lately? Toward an Investment Theory of Voting." *American Political Science Review* 70, no. 3 (1976): 779–805.

Primeau, Ronald. *The Rhetoric of Television.* New York: Longman, 1979.

RePass, David E. "Issue Salience and Party Choice." *American Political Science Review* 65, no. 2 (1971): 389–400.

Riskind, John H., and Wilson, David W. "Interpersonal Attraction for the Competitive Person: Unscrambling the Competition Paradox." *Journal of Applied Social Psychology* 12, no. 6 (1982): 444–52.

Robinson, Michael J. "American Political Legitimacy in an Era of Electronic Journalism: Reflections on the Evening News." In *Television as a Social Force: New Approaches to TV Criticism,* ed. D. Cater and R. Alder, 29–49. New York: Praeger, 1975.

———. "Television and American Politics." *The Public Interest* 48 (1977): 1–40.

Roper Organization. *Trends in Attitudes toward Television and Other Media: A Twenty-Four Year Review.* New York: Television Information Office, 1983.

Rosenberg, Shawn; Bohan, Lisa; McCafferty, Patrick; and Harris, Kevin. "The Image and the Vote: The Effect of Candidate Presentation on Voter Preference." *American Journal of Political Science* 30, no. 1 (1986): 108–27.

Rosenfeld, Lawrence, and Civikly, Jean M. *With Words Unspoken.* New York: Holt, Rinehart, Winston, 1976.

Rossi, Peter H. "Four Landmarks in Voting Research." In *American Voting Behavior,* ed. E. Burdick and A.J. Brodbeck, 5–54. New York: Free Press, 1959.

Rusbult, C.E.; Johnson, D.J.; and Morrow, C.D. "Impact of Couple Patterns of Problem Solving on Distress and Nondistress in Dating Relationships." *Journal of Personality and Social Psychology* 50, no. 3 (1986): 744–53.

Sabato, Larry J. *The Rise of Political Consultants.* New York: Basic Books, 1981.

Steck, Loren; Levitan, Diane; McLane, David; and Kelley, Harold H. "Care, Need, and Conceptions of Love." *Journal of Personality* and *Social Psychology* 43, no. 3 (1982): 481–91.

Stevens, Paul. *I Can Sell You Anything.* New York: Ballantine Books, 1972.

Stokes, Donald E., and Miller, Warren E. "Party Government and the Saliency of Congress." *Public Opinion Quarterly* 26, no. 4 (1962):531–46.

Stone, Arthur A., and Neale, John M. "Effects of Severe Daily Events on Mood." *Journal of Personality and Social Psychology* 46, no. 1 (1984): 137–44.

Tedin, Kent, and Murray, Richard. "Public Awareness of Congressional Representatives: Recall versus Recognition." *American Politics Quarterly* 7, no. 4 (1979):509–17.

Tichnor, P.J., Donohue, G.A.; Olien, C.N. "Mass Media Flow and Differential Growth in Political Knowledge." *Public Opinion Quarterly* 34, no. 2 (1970): 159–70.

Tuckel, Peter. "Length of Incumbency and the Reelection Chances of U.S. Senators." *Legislative Studies Quarterly* 8 (May 1983): 283–88.

Vogler, David J. *The Politics of Congress.* 4th ed. Newton, Mass.: Allyn and Bacon, 1981.

Westlye, Mark C. "Competitiveness of Senate Seats and Voting Behavior in Senate Elections." *American Journal of Political Science* 27, no. 2 (1983):253–83.

White, G.L. "Physical Attractiveness and Courtship Progress." *Journal of Personality and Social Psychology* 39, no. 3 (1980): 660–68.

White, Theodore Harold. *The Making of the President 1960.* New York: Pocket Books, 1961.

Wiggins, Jerry S.; Wiggins, Nancy; and Conger, Judith Cohen. "Correlates of Heterosexual Somatic Preference." *Journal of Personality and Social Psychology* 10, no. 1 (1968):82–90.

Wolfinger, Raymond E., and Rosenstone, Stephen J. *Who Votes?* New Haven: Yale Univ. Press, 1980.

Wright, Charles. *Mass Communication: A Sociological Perspective* 2nd ed. New York: Random House, 1975.

Zukin, Cliff. "Mass Communication and Public Opinion." In *Handbook of Political Communication*, ed. D. Nimmo and K. Sanders, 359–90. Beverly Hills: Sage, 1981.

Index

Videostyle in Senate Campaigns was designed by Sheila Hart; composed by G&S Typesetters, Austin, Texas; and printed and bound by Braun-Brumfield, Ann Arbor, Michigan. The book was set in 10/13 Bookman Light with Caslon 224 Bold display and printed on 60-lb. Glatfelter.